Middle School Years Without Tears

Getting Ready (At Any Time) for Wonderful, ***Awesome***, Successful, and ***Thrilling*** Middle School Experiences!

By Lizabeth Jenkins-Dale, M.Ed.

ISBN: 1453806490
ISBN-13: 9781453806494
Library of Congress Control Number: 2010913561

A wise and informative book. As I read the book my heart was touched by Lizabeth's sincerity to share her experience as both a parent and teacher of the middle school years to stay focused on positive outcomes. This book is to be read carefully as a guide for planning events, activities, budgets, schedules and contacts. Most importantly it invites and offers us inspiration and encouragement to be appreciative of the opportunity to become co-creators of solutions with this middle school aged youth. A powerful challenge to support our teens during the time of their rapid growth of self-identity and self-esteem.

– Barbara Borom, PhD
Counselor, Integral Health Educator
www.spiritabundant.com

Also authored:

Creating and Managing for **Wonderful**, ***Awesome***, *Successful*, and ***Thrilling*** Middle School Experiences! (2011)

More Stuff for **Wonderful**, ***Awesome***, *Successful*, and ***Thrilling*** Middle School Experiences! (2012)

Choose, Groove, Move (2011)

Additional Information:

Additional information about the author, getting ready for wonderful, awesome, successful, and thrilling middle school experiences, and other topics can be found at these two interactive websites:

www.lizabethjenkinsdale.com
www.middleschoolyearswithouttears.com

DEDICATION

This first book of three is dedicated to
my middle school aged daughter,
who emanates her goodness,
her internal wisdom,
and her perfect definition about life every day.

In 1971, John Lennon asked the world if it could imagine a world filled with peace. John was right. Peace does begin in our imaginations and is absolutely obtainable everywhere, even in middle schools. The world has just been going about it in an unproductive way. However, change is constantly happening.

PREFACE

For the past ten years, I have been a student of numerous leading edge authors who are joyfully participating in Earth's magnificent and perfect progression. My "book angels" have been very busy leading me to sources of information at the precise moment I was ready for it. It is awe inspiring to look back and see the material that just happened to be given to me or got my attention by literally falling off the bookshelf or simply caught my eye. Sometimes, it was only a passage or two to be read in the moment, but most times, it was a book to purchase and treasure forever. As my bookcase collection grew, so did my knowledge and understanding of the contents found on all the pages.

Also in those ten years, relevant people entered my life with pertinent messages. Some presented information that felt awkward and foreign, thus creating a movement toward information that freely resonated with my spirit. I am thankful for both types of persons because the discomfort of one type developed my intense motivation to find the other. People and books, combined with life experiences, have produced in me my profound knowing – my Truth, for which I am eternally grateful.

Acknowledging I did not get to this point alone, I wish to express my deepest gratitude to these cutting edge leaders (in alphabetical order): Ted Andrews, Karen Berg, Dr. Barbara J. Borom, Dr. Joan Borysenko, Rhonda Byrne, Dr. Richard Carlson, Dr. Deepak Chopra, April Crawford, Dr. Wayne W. Dyer, Betty J. Eadie, Dr. Masaru Emoto, Debbie Ford, Esther and Jerry Hicks, Napoleon Hill, Dr. Meg Blackburn Losey, Louise Hay, Dr. Barbara Maxx Hubbard, Dr. Spencer Johnson, Sue Monk Kidd, Dr. Ihaleakala Hew Len, Michael Murphy, Bob Proctor, don Miguel Ruiz, Rose Marie Swanson, Eckhart Tolle, James Twyman, James Van Praagh, Dr. Doreen Virtue, Dr. Joe Vitale, and Neale Donald Walsh.

The contents on the pages of the *Middle School Years Without Tears* book series is my interpretation of what I amassed through personal conversations, absorbed from numerous books and other materials, and ascertained in the course of life experiences.

My focus is on all the children already present on Earth, including the Indigo, Crystal, Star, Rainbow, and the many other incredible children arriving on Earth moment by moment. It is my intention to assist parents to higher levels of understanding so all children can be raised in such ways that they reach for their highest purpose and potential. Breaking away the old shell of the parenting paradigm is, indeed, part of the Earth changes we are all going through. It is about new structure and positive ways to view parenting. This fresh way of parenting will give you the best of both worlds—happy parents and well-balanced children. (This paragraph excerpted from *The Akashic Records* per Rose Marie Swanson[1], May 26, 2010)

With tremendous wonderment, with intriguing awe, with personal success, and with great thrill, I thank all the influences that helped me write the three books in the *Middle School Years without Tears* series.

CONTENTS

INTRODUCTION

One recent morning I had a vivid dream teaching a language arts lesson at the beginning of the year to very typical students in a very typical school. I presented the process humans utilize to start forming sounds for communication. The whole class mouthed "Ba ba ba" and "Da da da" to notice that the mouth goes up and down. A pretty fun and non-complex movement of the mouth, so no wonder these sounds are usually first! After I waited for the loud, student-led, and exaggerated "BA BA BA" and "DA DA DA" efforts to calm down, I was just about to explain how humans put sounds together to form words when I woke from my slumber. Pondering my incredibly real dream, I recognized two very important things all over again: (1) that I really do love middle school children, all of them—the sneaky ones, the obnoxious ones, the call out ones, the talking back ones, the "I'm not going to do what she says" ones, the shy ones, the social ones, the over-achieving ones, the "I'm just gonna shrug my shoulders" ones, the "I don't care about learnin' nuthin" ones, the "I'm just going to sit here" ones, the instantly likeable ones, the "I'm going to try really hard" ones, the "I'm going to move to that seat near my friend and see if the teacher notices" ones, the "I'm gonna say funny things" ones, the "I'm gonna do distracting things like stick a pencil up my nose" ones, and so on, and (2) that there will always be teachers around the world trying their best to teach the variety of middle school students mentioned. There is much we can do to prepare all children for wonderful, awesome, successful, and thrilling middle school experiences, and to positively harness all that variety. So now, without further delay, on to…m…mi…mid…middle…

Well, your little one is not so little anymore, and it is time for … come on… you can say it… MIDDLE SCHOOL! It does not matter if your child already has completed one or two, or even is finished with these years. Middle school can be a wonderful, awesome, successful, and thrilling experience any time.

Would it be great if we could just be like some other cultures and totally skip the adolescent stage of life? Upon a previously agreed age, all young females and males become adults. Done. One day you are a child; the next day you are an adult ready to be married, have children, and take on leadership roles. It appears this system works for them, or at least that is what I observe through the TV documentaries.

I have always been intrigued by this manner of becoming an adult, and have evaluated the pros and cons of such a quick life change. Are those who turn the specified age all really ready for it? Are there some who are terrified, but cannot show emotion because of culture pressure and, therefore, deny their true feelings? Do they carry this burden around with them all their lives? Are there some who just cannot quite be the adult that the culture expects and is ousted because of it? If the answers to these questions turn out to be yeses, then our societies and cultures have more similarities than differences.

Regardless of the speed or cultural customs of any society, the young grow up knowing the older members expect the younger members to eventually assume the societal responsibilities. Making this a smooth transition is beneficial to all. This transition begins way before adolescence.

Much parenting effort goes into starting children "on the right foot" in the pre-school and elementary years. Parents are especially involved and are attentive to homework, friends, activities, and communication with teachers. Many parents diminish this involvement when their children attend middle school. Perhaps, it is because the parents are burned out. It could be because there are other siblings to care for. It might be because parents perceive middle school as a time to let go. It could be because middle schools inadvertently make parents feel "out of the loop." It might be because middle school children push parents away as peers are preferred. No matter the cause or reason for reduced parental involvement, middle school is not a time to let go, but to remain diligent with parenting. Things do change, however, *how* one performs the parenting.

This book series, *Middle School Years Without Tears*, offers parents opportunity: Can parents believe that middle school does not have to be the dreaded years? That middle school does not have to be awful? That middle school can be fun? That middle schoolers can get through the middle school years with smiles? I will admit that the title may be a bit adventuresome. There might be some tears, but those tears can be wonderful portals for positive life lessons.

The suggestions and ideas presented in these books are derived from seventeen years of teaching in Pennsylvania and South Carolina public schools. I taught first grade two years, second grade four years, fifth grade one year, sixth grade two years, and seventh grade eight years. So, ten of my seventeen years were teaching middle school students. That is nearly two thousand days' experience!

Cultural diversity has been the focus of our country for decades now. All the schools where I have been employed primarily educate two races: African Americans and Caucasians. Other races composed a small percentage of the student body. I do believe that all middle school students, no matter the race, culture, religion, or sex have similar desires: to be accepted, understood, respected, and successful. So, please adapt the contents of this book for your particular child's background.

My unique educational path cannot be denied as an important and positive influence on these books. I attended public schools until third grade. From this point forward, my education was completed in several private schools: grade school to eighth grade, high school, Grove City College, Pennsylvania (B.A.), and University of Charleston, South Carolina (M.Ed.). It is not that my parents suddenly disliked public education and moved me to a private school when I was eight years old. Not so! My sister attended public schools for many years. My parents' wisdom told them that one size does not fit all, so they searched for other educational avenues for me. They observed that I needed opportunity to socially mature before continuing with my academics even though my grades were well above average. My parents switched me to a private school to assist with the transition as I repeated third grade, which allowed me to catch up socially. Now I was older and taller, as well as very knowledgeable of the third grade curriculum. The confidence I gained that year was invaluable. I am eternally grateful for this switch, as the change turned out to be exactly what I needed. There are many paths to a great education and parent involvement is necessary at every step of the way for each child. One size *does not* fit all.

In addition to my educational background and teaching experience, another influencing factor is that I am a proud middle school mom myself. Being on this side of the middle school experience has been interesting. I have a new perspective of some of the parent frustrations. Although my daughter's school does an excellent job with parent communication, this was the first time I felt out of the loop. Previously being a teacher, I always had a source for the "inside scoop." In my second book, *Creating and Managing for Wonderful, Awesome, Successful, and Thrilling Middle School Experiences,* I address how to maintain and promote positive communication with the vast group of those involved with middle school.

My personal parenting philosophy definitely contributes to the suggestions and ideas presented in these books as well. I believe that all children come hardwired with goodness. I believe that all children are born with an internal personal wisdom that, when honored, creates harmony for all. I believe the parental role is to assist children with the start of their lives while allowing them to follow their own life paths. While acknowledging this philosophy is somewhat divergent from other parenting styles, such as the traditional top down parenting (parent belief system dictates all until child is 18 years old), I do recognize the comfort, for both parents and children, of reasonable parental boundaries and the necessity of loving parental guidance. I believe the parenting purpose is to positively support children so that they remember who they really are: good, positive, creative, intelligent, and wonderful beings on life journeys.

On these pages, you will find suggestions that are unique and provide new perspectives. The purpose of this book is to give parents fresh ideas in supporting their children in any middle school for all levels in all areas. The middle school years referenced in this book are the years after elementary school and prior to high school. No matter how your school is organized or labeled (junior high, intermediate, or middle), this book contains much useful information for you. The audience of this book is assumed to be parents of regular education students, or students who have at least partial exposure and involvement with regular education. While I do have some experience with special education students, I do not feel qualified to address these students' needs directly. Again, topics discussed on these pages can be adjusted to suit your child.

Parents of homeschooled children will benefit reading this book to obtain an understanding of those in public education. Homeschooled children interact with students enrolled in public schools and can benefit knowing about these children's experiences. Also, no matter the manner in which one receives education, all children and all parents desire lives filled with happiness, fun, and peace. This book discusses how to have such lives.

Parents of private school students can glean helpful ideas as well. Private schools tend to have smaller teacher to student ratios, but still have middle school group dynamics. Many public and private schools have similar issues, such as beginning school jitters, with which *Getting Ready for Wonderful, Awesome, Successful, and Thrilling Middle School Experiences* can assist.

I have written this book as if I am talking with you, the parents. So, it is a dialogue! I tried to anticipate your reactions and questions to the material presented. These interactions and comments are highlighted in boxes within the text.

"You mean like this? When the reader sees a box like this one, it contains parent interactions with you, the author? It is what you thought would be a parent's reaction to what you have written?"

Yes. Just like that! You will see these text boxes intermittently throughout this book and the other two books in this series.

"Why are there three books? Why not just write one big book?"

There is so much to middle school that one big book could be overwhelming. So I split it into three parts. The one you are holding in your hands, *Getting Ready (At Any Time) for Wonderful, Awesome, Successful, and Thrilling Middle School Experiences,* is the first book of three in the *Middle School Years Without Tears* series. You have at your fingertips many ideas and perspectives for the time up to the first day of school. The second book subtitled, *Creating and Managing For Wonderful, Awesome, Successful, and Thrilling Middle School Experiences*, provides an invaluable and thorough description of a typical teacher's day and a behind-the-scenes look at the typical student's day. Why? So you will be enlightened what your child and child's teachers may experience on a daily basis. You will be surprised by a few things. The second book includes all the different types of school communications, including parent to parent, parent to principal, parent to vice principal, parent to teacher, parent to community, student to teacher, and student to student, as well as suggestions for optimal and positive communication for each type. In addition, there are strategies for what to do when your child is not performing as academically well as you know your child could.

Finally, *More Stuff for Wonderful, Awesome, Successful, and Thrilling Middle School Experiences* contains techniques for taking tests, descriptions of and approaches for the vast types of middle school socialization, strategies for your child to handle conflicts, ideas for students who need to release some extra, pressurized emotions, and techniques for you, the parent, to enrich your own life. If you are happy, fulfilled, prosperous, and healthy, you will be in a better position to be an awesome parent. In the last book, there is a section just for you!

These books are *not* comprehensive manuals for parents of middle schoolers because the subject, students, schools, geographic regions, state requirements, and unique personalities of schools are far too vast to cover every aspect completely. I am quite skeptical of any book claiming to be comprehensive especially when it comes to middle school. The topics discussed, however, can be easily applied and adapted to the middle school in your neck of the woods. It is my intention to provide you sound suggestions, practical strategies, and logical rationale for the suggestions and strategies to make middle school a wonderful, awesome, successful, and thrilling experience for *all* those involved. I believe you will find the suggestions and strategies empower any child to control the experiences instead of the experiences controlling the child. I also believe that these universal suggestions and strategies can be applied toward every aspect of your child's middle school experience. They work on everything!

So, take your ten to fourteen year old child to school and watch him or her get on the middle school roller coaster with such tremendous enthusiasm as only a child of this age can exhibit. These next few years are an exhilarating ride. It is a fantastic time in your child's life, and yes, it can be filled with wonderful, awesome, successful, and thrilling experiences!

Happy Reading!
Lizabeth Jenkins-Dale, M.Ed.
September 2010

ONE

Yikes! I Am a Middle School Parent!

> *[Sweaty hands, nervous stomach.] "I think I am going to throw up! Ugh! I don't want to let go of what is familiar to me! What's it going to be like? My head hurts. There's too much for my brain to think about. Oh, I just can't believe it's time for... MIDDLE SCHOOL!!"*

And I'm not even writing about the kids yet! Relax, parents! I will show you how to ease into middle school and celebrate with an eighth grade graduation.

Some parents dread middle school. But not the students. Most are really curious and interested in moving into this new time of their lives. Believe it or not, middle school years have a purpose. That purpose is to begin the process of asserting these growing human beings into happy adults who are joyfully reaching for their highest purposes and potentials. Some people cannot or do not want to think of their little one as an adult, but…

It is going to happen anyway, so we might as well embrace the process. After all, didn't you go through the process? Good or bad, we all went through the transition to adulthood. This adolescence stage is just as important as the others. I strongly encourage you to think, speak, act, and sing a positive song of what the middle school years can be.

Middle school can be:

- An opportunity to seek and find one's identity
- An opportunity to discover and develop talents
- A time of tremendous growth in all areas
- A time of incredible fun for all those involved, even the parents
- A smooth journey to pre-adulthood

"A smooth journey to pre-adulthood? Are you nuts? Do you know what my best friend said, whose kid was in eighth grade last year? He had the worst time of his life! His mother is soooo glad it's over."

"The teachers just picked on my daughter. She had a difficult time making friends. Her self-esteem went down the drain."

"I didn't recognize my child the whole way though middle school. In fact, I really didn't like him. I just couldn't wait to until middle school was over."

"Every day was difficult. My daughter came home crying a lot. Things eventually improved, but it was really tough the first year."

Yeah, I know. I KNOW! I have heard story after story during the many years I taught middle school. It was frustrating at times, yet I loved it deep down inside. It was a challenge every moment. There were plenty of days when I really, really wanted to quit.

I enjoyed watching people's reactions when I told them about my career. They searched me for any remnants of sanity for *choosing* to be a middle school teacher. So, I have heard and experienced the stories of middle school. Believe me…trust me…middle school can be a really positive experience and a lot of your child's experience depends on you.

You get what you focus on. Focus on the negatives about middle school and you will set your child up for a hard time. Focus on the excitement of this age and you will set your child up for a wonderful experience. The initial success of your child depends on you.

"WHAT? You've written that twice in this book of yours! *I* am responsible?"

Yes, and I mean it. Much of the success of your child depends on you. Do not be alarmed by this claim. It is a good claim! Middle school students also have responsibility for their successes too. Simply understand that there is much you can easily do to promote the success of your child.

The most important effort you can make is this: feel, talk, and be excited about middle school. If you hear, think, and talk about the negatives of middle school, what messages are you sending to your child, even before she gets there, currently is there, or was there? If you hear, think, and talk about the positives of middle school, what messages are you sending to your child, even before he gets there, currently is there, or was there? Which is a great vision to send to your child of the middle school possibilities? No matter if your child is just starting, already in middle school, or finished with middle school, expressing the positives of middle school can create wonderful, awesome, successful, and thrilling middle school experiences at any time. Isn't this good news? If your child is preparing for middle school, I will show you how to pre-pave the road for your child even years ahead of the middle school experience.

> "Great. Now I have more guilt. I should have been preparing my child years ago?"

Awesome! You are now aware! That is always preferred to *not* being aware. But, absolutely no guilt will be found here or anywhere else in this book. This is a guilt-free book. If you are aware of any negativity, I will show how you can start right now to switch to being positive about middle school. It is never too late.

The best way to make change occur is to BE the change. Mahatma Gandhi, an advocate of non-violent resistance, was right when he said, "You must be the change you wish to see in the world." Gandhi knew and understood that change starts with the self. Otherwise, people will wait in vain for others to change first. To focus on the positive will not require as much effort as you might think. It will be perceived as effortless once you ponder the wonderful benefits of this focus. Can you imagine your child leaving each day with a skip in her walk as she eagerly waits for the bus? Can you imagine your son smiling because his homework is complete for the night and he knows he is being successful? How about visualizing your child's smile with friends or receiving positive communication from your child's teachers because your child is happy, agreeable, cooperative, and pleasant? Imagine all the possibilities for your child! To get these imaginations to become realities, amazingly very little needs to be done.

It might help you to imagine all the possibilities for your child if we described a middle school student. Hmmmm…OK…um…well… describe a middle school student? Let's see…gosh!...uhhhhhh. It is really a tough job to solidify middle school student traits, but I make an attempt in the next section. It is in no way a conclusive description, but it might give you something new to ponder.

TWO

What Is a Middle Schooler Anyway?

A single definition of middle school students does not exist. The diversity is what makes this age so incredible and memorable. Allow me to entertain you with a few middle school stories that will demonstrate diversity!

There was a student who accepted a dare and five bucks to stick his hand into an ant pile for thirty seconds. If you have ever lived in the South, you know what I am referring to and know just how painful even one ant bite can be. He received the five dollars, fame for a day, and a trip to the doctor's office with his very upset mother.

One day I looked up to see a student hanging on the top edge of the classroom door with one hand as the door swung back and forth. Amazingly, he hung there for a long time! The child made great efforts to entertain those walking to their next class.

It was very interesting how females would accessorize with whatever uniform regulation leeway they could create. One girl in particular wore canary yellow dangly earrings, multiple brightly colored bangle bracelets on each wrist, neon colored shoe laces with socks to match, and, to complete the ensemble, five belts, all...you guessed it...brightly colored! These accessories definitely overshadowed the khaki pants and blue shirt uniform. So much for making all the kids dress alike.

There was a group of boys who created and presented the most wonderful simile poetry about feces...with props...OK, they were fake props, but still! It was a performance to remember.

Another memory is of a female student, who made a huge discovery during the science genetics unit. The teacher demonstrated Punnett Squares, a simplified method using boxes to explain the probability for parents' offspring to have certain traits such as eye shape, hair color, and, yes, sex organs. The probability of a child having male or female sex organs, is always 50 percent for male and 50 percent for female. Always. Every time. Using Punnett Squares, one can prove the 50-50 probability. In response to this information, the female student suddenly exclaimed out loud, "I thought it was who was on top that made a boy or girl!!"

One day, a middle school student brought a rather large sheet cake to school to share with her friends at lunch. There was quite a commotion with the cake, so a few teachers went over to investigate the situation. Was it her birthday? No. Was it a friend's birthday? No. It was her deceased baby brother's birthday.

Middle school students are industrious when it comes to money. A student made flip books on sticky note pads to sell so that when the buyer rapidly flipped the pages, the character drawn on each page "moved." I am not sure if his homework was done, but he was making money.

So many memories with candy! Noticing circular candy rolling on the floor during class after falling from a student's lap, hearing candy wrapping being opened during class, watching students slip candy into their mouths with pretend yawns and continuing the charade into fully extended arm stretches, or observing students "smoking" candy. How? The students crush a thin roll of small candies creating a sweet powder inside the wrapper. If they suck in just right after making a small hole at one end of the wrapper, students can puff out rings of "smoke" in the air.

Students love to divert the teacher's attention from the curriculum. I got very good not flinching after hearing verbal distractions, loud noises, odorous bodily functions, or unique physical body twisting. I kept on teaching after such occurrences. Students watched for my reaction. With not much to see from me, perhaps this made them try harder??? One distraction that was performed without fail every year by a handful of students involved placing an assortment of school supplies in a variety of ways on body parts during instructional time—pens or markers in ears, both ears; pencil eraser replacements suctioned to chins, foreheads, tongues, and noses; pencils or markers up noses, both nostrils; markers rolled between noses and lips; scissor handle openings on noses, ears, and tongues; stickers on eyelids and chins, masking tape on mouths, around heads, and dangling from chins like a beard; paper triangles or "claws" taped to ends of fingers; and more…oh, so much more!

There was a student who took school supplies to a whole new level—an internal level. The second day of school, this student snuffed a piece of yarn up his nose with the intention of pulling it out through his mouth. When he attempted to pull it out (whole hand in mouth), he vomited. This student retrieved his piece of yarn from the purged semi-liquid spew on the floor and displayed the dripping wet prize for the class with the most triumphant grin I have ever seen.

Every now and then, I would see thumb sucking during class, even when I taught seventh grade. And, yes, it was both sexes. These students did not really care if others saw them thumb sucking.

Snoring and drooling while sleeping in class, although rare, did occasionally happen. They could not get away with it for long because snoring in class is easily heard and very distracting. The occasional pool of drool on the desk created quite a stir, too—pretty gross to teachers, but completely amusing to middle school students.

Gum chewing was rampant in all the schools in which I taught. We teachers tried to curb it, but were never successful. If caught, the students were told to get rid of the gum, which meant (in our minds) they would get up to spit the gum into the nearest trash can…quietly.

But, nooooo! Students had different gum removal ideas and demonstrated them frequently, such as opting to swallow their gum instead. Of course, the swallowing process would be exaggerated with loud gulping, theatrical head dipping, and last, but not least, pronounced chest pounding, to assist the gum down the esophagus. Then, the students would eagerly and voluntarily open their mouths wide open with, "AHHHHHH" so teachers could conduct mouth checks. Eeewww! Why we teachers addressed gum chewing over and over is a wonder!

Middle school students really get into projects. This makes it fun for teachers too. One year, my students created commercials with props. Some groups zoomed over the top with effort and creativity! There was a group of boys who devised a sports car commercial. The boys made several car prototypes from cardboard boxes. The finished products were incredibly detailed with all the features one would expect in a sports car...knobs, gauges, a sound system, wheels, keys, windows, and more! During the commercial and before I could say anything, the boys "drove" the cars all the way down the long school hallway. Can you imagine the commotion this caused as the boys test drove their cars in the hallway?

Middle school girls seem to love writing on their bodies with whatever they have...pens, markers, pencils, nail polish, or lip gloss. Why? I do not know. I have read friend's phone numbers, reminders, boyfriend names, class notes, and homework assignments on the arms of female students. Read your child's skin. You just might learn something about your daughter! Skin is, in addition to writing paper, art paper. All kinds of shapes have been found on female arms, especially hearts. The more hearts you see, the more you can be certain there is a crush. It is pretty incredible what a child can create during a whole day of middle school—unique designs using lines, spots, waves, and colored markers. Too bad it gets erased in the shower. Ah, but we are not done yet. No, not yet! Skin is also a surface for games. I have seen tic-tac-toe, dot, and word games played on precious, young skin. So, is it foolish or good use of resources? I think the answer to that question depends on your age.

I can vividly remember a group of boys, who were supposed to be moving to their next class, having a glitter battle in my classroom. As a language arts teacher, I used many different activities and substances, such as glitter, to enhance the writing experience. These boys switched the enhanced writing experience to an uncomfortable writing experience…for days. The four boys were totally covered with gold glitter. I mean *totally* covered! They stayed behind and cleaned the desks and floor. My initial reaction quickly changed to humor as it took them a looooong time to clean my room. They had immense amounts of glitter in their hair, binders, ears, and yes, in their pants. From what I heard later in the day, glitter in one's pants is uncomfortable to say the least. Even the next day, I heard they were still quite… um…irritated.

It is not only the students who create silly, unforgettable, and often, embarrassing middle school moments. Teachers do it too! One year, I honestly and mistakenly said "orgasm" for "organism" while teaching science. What NOT to say with hormonal seventh grade students!! They thoroughly enjoyed the color of my face turning a bright red as I desperately tried to gain my composure and continue with class. Unfortunately, the rest of the lesson was shot as I heard miscellaneous giggling at varied intervals. I was pretty glad to get home and put some time between that incident and me!

At another time I was experiencing an abnormal amount of gas build up in my intestine. Yes, everyone gets flatulence. It is a normal part of life! I am not sure of the cause, but in the middle of the lesson I was experiencing the effect. I tried hard to deal with the situation as best as I could. What is a teacher to do? We cannot just put the kids on hold and run to the bathroom. If there is no one in the hallway to snag to cover the classroom, we are stuck. S-T-U-C-K…STUCK! So finally, the bell rang and immediately there is loud commotion. Yes! I could finally deal with the gas build up and no one would know. As I gave directions for the end of day preparations, no one heard me take care of my problem. Pretty soon, however, not far from me, a kid exclaimed in an extremely loud voice, "WHAT IS THAT STINK?!?!" I looked at him, trying to control the guilty smile forthcoming from my lips, but before I could say anything, another boy was already accusing *him* of creating the smell. The first boy started to defend himself, and of course, the two of them got into a verbal battle over who made the stink. I, meanwhile, could hardly keep a straight face as I walked toward the door…feeling less bloated and just plain ol' giddy.

For some reason, teachers love popcorn. It is fun to follow the buttery smell to the source and get a handful of popped kernels. At least once a year, a teacher throws the popcorn bag into the microwave then runs to the bathroom with good intentions of returning in time to monitor the popping. But, it doesn't always work out perfectly. So outside everyone has to go because the fire alarm sounded and the fire department is on its way. It is pretty embarrassing when there is no emergency and one person caused great inconvenience to many, all because someone was simultaneously peeing and popping corn kernels.

I have never been able to forget the story about a teacher's panties appearing in the school hallway. It was a payday Friday, which meant teachers were allowed to wear jeans. When this teacher dressed for work Friday morning, she apparently slipped the jeans back up her body from the same spot she removed them the previous night. A colleague's curiosity was heightened when she found dainty, sexy panties with sparkly design in the hallway. It was not what school students usually wear! This colleague must have made quite a loud comment because the now red-faced owner of the panties quickly appeared to collect her personal garment. Apparently, the panties fell from one of her pant legs. Fortunately, this happened prior to the start of the school day, but not prior to a colleague finding the wayward panties.

Humanness permeates middle school. Messing up abounds! Students mess up. Teachers mess up. Principals mess up. Receptionists mess up. The building messes up too!

Yup! Buildings can do their part in creating interesting middle school days. It is guaranteed to have a fire alarm go off when the temperature outside drops and heaters are turned on for the first time of the season. All that collected dust from months and months of non-use just loves to smoke!

I will never forget the first day of middle school one year when, for no apparent reason, the electricity failed…for hours. The sun was shining. It was a beautiful day. No rain or storm cloud in sight. Why did the electricity fail? Who knows, but it was a very memorable day as I reviewed beginning of school information with emergency lights only.

All these events are no different than the many middle schoolers who have had interesting days doing embarrassing things (tripping coming up the stairs with papers flying everywhere), having difficult experiences with peers (arguing over bumping in the hall) or teachers (forgetting homework), and being frustrated with academics (feeling like the only one who doesn't understand). Lots happen in middle school each and every day. A lot happens a lot! And they *love* to share it!

Expect stories. Expect *very interesting* stories! Keep these stories in perspective, however. The source is a creative middle school student! I promise you that just as parents hear stories from students about teachers, teachers hear all kinds of stories about parents. I have heard pretty incredible untrue or half true stories. Teachers know to take these stories with a grain of salt, depending on the content and how it is told.

So, with all those middle school stories fresh in your mind, we will go back to the original question: What is a middle schooler anyway? The question has vast, unending, and multiple possibilities for answers, but here are some of them. A middle schooler might be a human being:

- Swinging between childhood and adulthood;

- Expressing with and without confidence utilizing a variety of ways to do so anyway;

- Dealing with a rapidly changing body at different intervals in non-balanced ways (e.g., feet large, but rest of body is not), and no one knows when the changes will occur;

- Dealing with new massive amounts of hormones dispersing throughout the body, thus resulting in emotional outbursts, odd behavior, and crazy ideas that surprise everyone, including the middle schooler;

- Trying to evaluate past choices and future choices independent of parents with only ten to fourteen years total life experience;

- Engaging peer input more than parent input;
- Questioning about accepting responsibility;
- Attempting to define himself/herself acutely for the first time;
- Creating an individual and personal code of conduct to interact with other human beings;
- Expressing oneself sexually to varying degrees in new ways;
- Contemplating the pros and cons of accepting and rejecting the sexual attention of another;
- Beginning to realize his/her own power; and/or
- Desiring to turn back to childhood and desiring move forward to adulthood at the same time.

"Whoa! That's a lot for a child this age!"

I still promise you that middle school can be filled with wonderful, awesome, successful, and thrilling experiences!

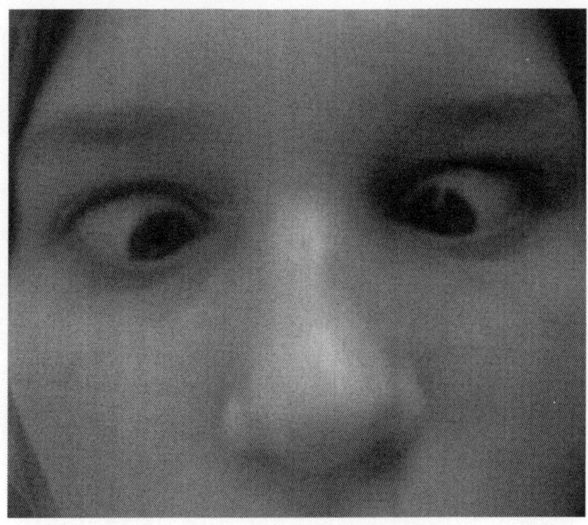

THREE

What's Fun about Middle School?

There is much fun about middle school—dances, boys, girls, games, lockers, multiple teachers, more peers in grade level, more independence, friends, school activities, new responsibilities, parties, and lots and lots and lots of silliness! I have seen numerous children thoroughly enjoy this time of life. They thrived! They bloomed! As my daughter commented about middle school, "It's going to be an adventure!" Her assessment is correct.

Parents can also enjoy this time of life with their children too. While still being very in tune with your child, you can experience a bit of independence from your child. You can experience humorous "craziness," as your child will entertain you with "creative" ideas and stories. You can experience an early adolescence party again as a chaperone. You can experience the wonderment that *your* parents experienced as you see your "baby" grow up, talk to so and so on the phone, and flirt with another. You can experience joy as you see your child develop friends, pursue academics, and start to realize her personality. It is all a matter of attitude. Do you want to see these things? Do you want to experience these things? If you do, you will embrace them!

The middle school experience is an experience of extremes—highs and lows, great days and not-so-good days—not often something in between. This is the reason parents are so important during the middle school years. You need to be the stable ones. One day your child loves so and so; the next day so and so is not really that cute. One day your child has a best friend; the next day they are not speaking to one another. One day your child will really enjoy a teacher; the next day your child will ask you to get him out of that teacher's class. Yes, they still view you as Superman and Wonder Woman, and they will be expecting that you can do this for them! There are many perplexing things you will observe during this wonderful time:

You may find your

- serious child lightening up a bit.
- quiet child coming out of his shell.
- totally-clueless-about-girls son smiling oddly when a girl is near. To quote my husband, "It's when boys are aware that girls are not just lumpy boys."
- usually calm daughter just cannot stay still for long, talks on the phone for hours, sends message after message electronically, and squeals a lot.
- playful child who has played basketball for fun is now playing with intensity.
- loving child who loved to give you hugs any time, any place will only do so in the privacy of your house.
- shy child wanting to attend a school dance.

- I-don't-care-how-I-look child suddenly requesting new, updated outfits.

- social child writing hearts, phone numbers, or designs on her arms.

- unobservant child noticing everything you wear, speak, or do, *and* telling you what to wear, say, or do.

- homebody child spending more time with peers than you.

- developing child demonstrating knowledge of new skills and learning that makes you realize that you now have just increased your pride way beyond what you thought was possible.

- sensible daughter in a group of jumping and screaming girls.

- intelligent son saying things like "I dunno", "Yup", and "Yeah."

You may find yourself

- watching your young one get metal brackets cemented on every tooth in an orthodontist's office.

- standing at the shoe store purchasing amazingly large sneakers for your child.

- hearing really strange, off-topic comments. For example, after talking about dinner plans, you hear, "Dr. Seuss is cool," which is followed with the comment, "*That* was random."

- looking at your little darling "spazzing" with interesting arm and leg movements, which occur at odd intervals while a silly grin appears during and after the spazzing moments.

- receiving too much information too quickly from a high-pitched voice and are having a hard time following the story from your now verbose daughter when you ask a simple question.

You may discover your

- benevolent child, who always agreed with you before, now has an opinion all of her own.
- usually rational child crying due to a minor incident at school.
- "airy" child, who only did what he had to do, is now taking academics seriously.
- seriously academic child is now *not* taking academics very seriously.
- verbose child suddenly speaking new words and you have no clue what they mean, nor the context in which you heard them.
- charming young son at the end of a school day with multiple small ponytails all over his head. From his beaming smile, you instinctively know that he allowed some pretty girls to do this to his hair.

You may notice your child

- expressing great disdain at your attempts to use your child's *teenagy* words. (Of course, you will say them incorrectly.)
- rolling her eyes more often.
- huffing and puffing more.
- returning home with a totally orange colored hand with green dots with no rational reason why.

- chewing gum like a cow, blowing bubbles incessantly, and maintaining a positive gum supply even Fort Knox would envy.

Despite some sometimes humorous, sometimes irritating, sometimes mind-boggling events, middle school has so much to offer! It *is* fun and there are many things you can do to create a smooth transition to middle school.

FOUR

Handling Pre-Middle School Jitters (or Jitters Anytime)

No matter how confident your child is, he or she will have some concerns or wonderings about middle school. Be proactive and do a few simple things before school starts. Even if middle school is already in session or completed for the year, you can adapt and implement these in your current situation. What will work well for your child?

Plan a School Visit During the Summer

Schedule a thorough school visit during the summer prior to starting a new school. Make sure this is scheduled so someone from the school is available escort you and your child around the school's interior and grounds. This tour would be complete with meeting as many pertinent people as possible, such as the principal, vice principal, bookkeeper, receptionist, guidance counselor(s), day porter(s), and teachers. Although not twelve-month employees, guidance counselors and teachers do make occasional visits during the summer and, with scheduling this visit, you may be able to meet them as well.

By scheduling a time with the school, you will receive the positive reception you deserve and desire. During the summer, schools clean, organize, and plan. Principals, receptionists, bookkeepers, and other twelve-month employees, go on vacations. Teachers, sometimes from other schools, conduct summer trainings. Multiple workers repair major building issues or install upgrades. There is usually lots of activity happening in schools over the summer and most of it is quite unsightly. For these reason and more, call ahead to schedule a visit. I have entered a school unannounced and have not been received well. When I toured the building by myself, because the front office personnel were too busy to give me a tour, I stepped around boxes, desks, miscellaneous teacher items nearly blocking the path, large piles of swept dirt, bugs, accumulated dust, and tall stacks of chairs in the hallways. The experience gave me a very funny feeling and I really questioned whether or not I wanted my child to attend this school, when in reality the school had a positive reputation. Immediately, I called ahead and went to another school where I was well received and was given a personal tour. I enrolled my child that day.

> "But, don't you think that scheduling a visit is a way for them to 'put their best foot forward' or to hide how the school really is? I like surprise visits better so that nothing is fake."

It is not that by scheduling a visit, you give opportunity to hide flaws: you give the school personnel time to prepare a great experience for you. Do you want to see the school with all classroom items shoved in the hallways as the cleaning crew waxes the floors? It is a dusty and smelly job! Do you want to meet the principal after he or she has just moved books to the bookroom and is now dripping wet of perspiration? Do you want to miss the receptionist on a lunch break? Not hardly. You want a positive experience with friendly, clean people. You want an explanation for any dirt or apparent chaos. You want a relaxed person to greet you and to take you on a personal tour of the building. You want that person to listen as you talk about your child and your child's specific needs. You want to feel good about the school!

If needed, schedule a visit at the beginning of the summer and one close to the start of school. Jitters can surface again in the course of a summer vacation. A good, positive school will gladly offer tours. No need to feel uncomfortable about asking for this service.

Obtain a school map. They have these readily available because each room must post one showing emergency exits. A map simplifies a seemingly overwhelming new school building and can help with your child knowing the places she will need to go once school starts. If your child is already enrolled, ask for the schedule too. Then, you can plan your child's travels through the hallways to each class. There may be a few alterations needed once school starts because not all hallways are accessible at all times to all students. For example, if sixth graders go to lunch first, they will not be allowed to travel through the seventh grade hall, even if this is the easiest way to the cafeteria. Middle school students just are not quiet when traveling in groups and for this reason there may be restrictions on hallway travel. It is still a great idea to be very familiar with the school layout prior to the beginning of the year. I always have utilized school maps when starting to teach in new schools.

Inquire about a summer orientation. Most schools have such an event planned for rising sixth graders. Incoming, new seventh or eighth graders could attend the same event and glean important information as well.

Plan Your Child's School Involvement

During the school visit, be sure to ask to see a school yearbook. You can get a feel for the school by looking at the pictures. Is there a school pamphlet highlighting the sports and related arts offerings? What are the clubs or groups? These might include drama, yearbook, chess, jazz band, art, science, news team, step team, and choir. Encourage your child to pursue clubs or groups that meet during the summer months so your child knows a few friendly faces at the beginning of the year.

What are the sports groups available—football, volleyball, track, soccer, swimming, and cheerleading? What was the team's record the previous year? Find out how you contact the coaches.

What are the offered special areas, a.k.a. related arts or exploratory? These can include physical education, art, foreign languages, music, choir, strings, and computers. Some of these classes are required as standard curriculum, but some are selected by students. Which ones would your child like? Selecting these prior to the start of the school year avoids first day of school confusion. Why wait to the beginning of school to find out whether your child is in band or not? Middle school offices are flooded with schedule change requests when school starts. It usually takes time to correct schedules. Ensure your child's middle school start is a smooth one by reviewing her schedule prior to the first day of school.

Thinking about which classes, groups, or clubs your child would like to join will assist the preparation for middle school. Joining a group is a great way to quickly feel comfortable. If your child is a returning seventh or eighth grader, take a look at the options again. Is there something to experience before leaving middle school? Has your child ever wanted to be in theater? Drama Club might be a new adventure. Has your child ever wanted to help design the school's yearbook? Yearbook Club offers students opportunity to design eye-appealing pages, to write intriguing copy, and to learn book making. What about band? The sooner the better to learn an instrument! It is beneficial to have as many experiences in middle school as possible before high school, where involvement usually is more intense and focused.

Knowing a few friendly faces the first day of school is a wonderful way to create a positive middle school experience. Ask the principal or receptionist for suggestions. These key people in the school know the students very well and can guide you to positive students.

Think back to a time you started something new. Do you remember the relief when seeing a familiar face? Yes, a peer suggestion from the principal or receptionist is valuable input indeed!

> "Hey! I like these suggestions! My child and I can plan her middle school experience, and then evaluate the plan before school starts. Additional ideas may surface during the summer. Thanks!"

Discuss All the Components of Your Child's Life

A middle schooler's life has many components: academics, friends, school, family, and personal. Managing all of these components is a juggling act, especially if there are other siblings. Most middle school students will arrange for friend, school, and personal time without your help. Academics will be a priority depending on your child. If you plan together with your middle schooler how to manage all the components, it is more likely that all of them will get the attention and time they deserve.

Take a look at your daily schedule. How do you manage the components of *your* life? Explaining your strategies and thought processes may help model for your child how to manage his time. It also may be a great communication opportunity in case your child has a negative opinion about how you conduct your life. By discussing how you manage all the components of your life, you just might create and receive more appreciation and understanding from your child.

Everyone needs "down time." Your child may need help with transitioning from school to home just like you do when you come home from work. Discuss an established routine for your child after school. What will he eat for a snack and how much? What will she do once home? Do you expect a phone call at work from your child to indicate he is home? When will homework be done? Where? Since homework breaks are permissible, what constitutes a homework break? Is TV, radio, music, or friends allowed while completing homework? Designate a spot for completed homework for parent-child review. How will the child let you know what is for homework each night? If the school doesn't provide students with an agenda or daily planner, how is your child going to keep track of each subject's homework, future test dates, and project due dates? When will your child's book bag be prepared and placed by the front door prior to bedtime? When is bedtime? How will your child get awake in the morning? Who will get a shower first? Second? How will your child leave in the morning? Rushed? Calmly? With breakfast complete or eaten on the run? Who takes care of the animals? Are beds to be made? There are many considerations! Discussing these things prior to the beginning of middle school with your child will be most beneficial and will add to the peace within your household.

The first two weeks of school create havoc on the roads in the morning until traffic patterns settle. Allow for this and leave extra early for school to ensure a positive experience. Being late the first day of school is so not cool!

The social component is a must to consider for any middle school aged child. When is your child's social time? Which social activities are positive? Who can your child socialize with and where? What if the other child's parents are not home? Discuss and explain your thoughts about all of these things because social activities evolve as your child ages, and there may be younger or older siblings who are doing different social activities. What worked well for one child may not work well for another. Treat each child uniquely, as current events may change between the time one child was in middle school and when the next one is in middle school. Perhaps, you moved to a new area. This will have a powerful impact on socializing because everything and everyone is unknown. Honor the age, maturity development, and distinct personality of your child with these discussions. Communication is very important.

There is no need to hold back too severely or to push too quickly regarding your child's social time. Allow your child to lead the way while you guide her through the vast choices. There is an obtainable balance…an easy, calm, and natural balance to supporting your child with socializing. Once you find this good feeling balance with the activities you and your child both decide upon, you will relax while your child is with friends. You will enjoy the time your child is with friends because you know at a deep level that this is the best social activity for him for that particular moment in time.

Depending on your child, you may have to be proactive and help plan social time for your shy, quiet, and reserved child. Or, you may have to be proactive and help plan personal time for your gregarious, extroverted, and expressive child. Personal time is just as important as the other components of anyone's life, including the children who do not seem to have a stop button. It is essential for children to develop into self-reliant, critical thinking, and complete beings who know how wonderful they are at a deep level. Personal time allows for this development, or a remembering (re-membering) at the soul level. Unless one periodically gets off the roller coaster of life and spends time alone, how can these develop while interacting with all the stimuli of the exterior world? Personal time may include apparently doing nothing, having no time schedule for part of a day, doing whatever good feeling thing comes to mind, prayerful contemplation, meditating, listening to music, resting, daydreaming, coloring, journaling, baking cookies, exercising, painting, or singing.

> "Coloring? Meditating? Journaling? I just can't see middle schoolers wanting to do these things. Coloring seems elementary. Meditating and journaling seem "adultish." Also, I thought it was best to keep middle school aged children busy to keep them out of trouble."

Well…hmmm…year after year, I was always amazed with the poetry my students in middle school created. The depth of meaning, the insightful word choices, and the "adultish" wisdom contained within the poetic lines always astounded me. For many years, I submitted each and every poem to several poetic contests with great results.

Obviously, others agreed with me regarding these students' poetic talents! As a reward for participating in the contests and for reaching the required number of accepted students, I received a book of the accepted published poems. By reading the poems of other students in other schools in other states, it was clear that middle school students everywhere are capable of self-reflection, meditational thinking, and poetic expression at very deep levels. Meditation and journaling are different than poetry, but are additional ways to develop, remember, and express soul-level beliefs.

Try coloring anything with a multitude of materials such as crayons, colored pencils, or markers. A delightful silliness surfaces with each back and forth motion. There is something so satisfying about coloring. Perhaps, the mystery of coloring is best left as is, but here are a few offerings anyway as to why coloring is so therapeutic and a great personal time activity for anyone of any age. Coloring provides a sense of accomplishment in a short period of time. Draw a circle and color it. Presto! You have accomplished something. Hang it on your bulletin board as a reminder. Coloring presents one with simple choices—what shape, what color, which part to fill in first, what pressure, and which direction for coloring strokes. Also, we cannot forget that coloring provides temporary release from whatever is perceived as negative (a boring academic lecture, a verbal assault, or a huge decision to make) or overpoweringly positive (wedding plans, first date, or night before middle school). So, to summarize coloring in poetic form…Coloring: conveniently cheerful, calming, and comforting when considering the cloudy and confusing catastrophe capabilities of other co-creators! (Meaning there are some people, co-creators, who produce discord in their lives with which coloring would be beneficial.) How is that for some poetic consonance alliteration?

"OK, OK. Enough! Your considerable concentration on coloring was cuddly cute, but way too carefully and conscientiously corny. See? I can compose using alliteration too! Could you answer my last question about keeping kids busy without using literary devices, please?"

Sure! Just trying to be entertaining. Keeping kids busy—yes, I whole-heartedly agree if there is a balance of all of the components and an understanding regarding the unique personality of every child. Most middle schoolers need many activities. Bored children will find their own activities with or without parental guidance. I prefer with parental guidance! Keeping kids busy with positive activities that cater to all the parts of a middle schooler's life will greatly assist your child (and you) to keep focused on activities that enhance life, that create really "cool" memories, and allow only beneficial events, people, and situations. My parents kept my sister and me busy with school and extra-curricular activities while balancing all the other aspects of our lives, including family time.

Family is important. Period. There are many types of families. All types are considered family units. It is my belief that family units provide all members thorough dosages of unconditional love, support, peace, health, cleanliness, and guidance. Hopefully, your family unit is perceived as fun, loving, and a safe place where your middle schooler wants to be. However, you may notice your child's opinion changing about family time. Recognize it for what it is and avoid blaming or laying guilt for not wanting to spend time with the family, which will only reinforce a negative view. Rather, point it out and calmly ask for an explanation for the change. Sometimes, a child might not even notice that he is not spending as much time with his family as he used to. Mentioning this may bring him back into alignment with its importance. Maybe she is bothered about having to babysit younger family members so much that when it comes to family time, she is "burned out." Maybe he needs more focus on academics and he thinks it is OK to use family time to study. With a good, positive, and non-judgmental discussion between you and your child, the issue can be rectified.

Now that she is older, the components of her life will need adjusting, such as more social time. These adjustments do not mean eliminating components from her life, rather, something was added. It is important to explain how family time is still in your child's best interest *and* in terms she can understand. The family unit has been supporting her for eleven, twelve, or so years and will continue to do so for many, many years. Family will still be there when the friends are gone. Family will still be there through those bad days. The family will still be there before anything, during everything, and after all of it! The people in the family unit are much more dependable than friends, as middle school friends can be fickle. Family equals unconditional love—much more secure than peer love. One can always count on family through thick and thin, through bad hair days, through zits, through special person break-ups, through you-name-it, and more.

Discussing family using these words will remind middle schoolers the importance of family time. It is a time to regroup, renew, and remember their foundations. Family is the springboard, or jumping off point, for all life's adventures. Family is the place to return to after the adventure is done and while waiting for the next one. Family offers the basic need of belonging. From this first ring of belonging, middle schoolers can branch off and extend into the next ring of belonging—friends. Middle school aged children tend to have tunnel vision when it comes to their day-to-day lives. Reminding them of their foundation from time to time allows them to broaden that tunnel vision and remember all the components of their lives.

> "This is really cool! You sorta gave me 'permission' to keep family as a priority during these years instead of giving in to the stereotype that kids this age will ignore family values. By showing me how to give reasons for maintaining close family ties, I can now do this!"

Other benefits of family time can be more tangible, and tangible goods carry much value with a child of this age. Can you offer a social reward, like having a friend come along when attending, participating, and helping with a younger sibling's birthday party? How about a pizza party next weekend for him and his friends for putting on a smile at this weekend's Great Uncle Ned's eighty-eighth birthday party? Pizza is powerful, persuasive food! How about a shopping trip to the mall if she can help a younger brother study his spelling words willingly?

"Isn't this bribery? Kids are just supposed to do what they are told to do. Family time is important. Grades are important. Aren't you establishing a dependency on getting something for doing what is just required?"

Yes, I can see your point. If you have a super child, who does exactly what he is told, then none of that will be necessary. If you have a middle schooler whose values are the same as yours, then awesome! It has been my experience that this is a time when children of the middle school years start to think for themselves. They start to evaluate how they are living their lives from their perspectives instead of just absorbing the given parents' perspectives. They question your values and reasoning. This is wonderful because they are starting to become adults! They are starting to think independently! They are starting to establish their own code of living! They are critically thinking, which is essential to developing into successful, positive, and independent adults. So, while they are progressing through this process of being a critical thinker and evaluating Mom and Dad's values, they might need some incentives to keep focused on their true desire for peace, happiness, cooperation, and joy. They might need some incentives to attend some cousin's wedding on the same weekend as their best friends' big birthday party. It is not that your son compromised who he is by choosing family over friends. It is not that you forced your daughter to attend the wedding. But, your child decided to accept the incentive and attend the wedding all the while she is evaluating the family value because it keeps family peace, happiness, cooperation, and joy.

Children of any age want peace. Do not be fooled that middle school students like chaos. It is true human nature to want peace. Finding a way to "make it happen" during these years can be easier than you think. Get it? Easier than you *think*! Think there is a way. Think peace is possible every day with every situation.

A child who makes her bed every day does not always do it for the satisfaction of seeing the bed look neat and tidy. A child might make the bed because it has been asked of her and the reward of not having to hear a reminder about making her bed is worth the effort.

In other words...peace! Perhaps, it is worth completing homework on time to get a later curfew on Fridays. It is not necessarily the wonderful feeling of the homework being done, but the wonderful feeling of the reward. In other words...cooperation!

Students understand compromise, bribery, and persuasion very well. Middle school students are *masters* of these communication techniques! I would be rich if I had a penny for every time a student tried to bribe me to forgive a missed assignment, or give me a reason why he or she did not have to complete an assignment as directed, or offer a compromise with an assignment. Persuasion is the middle schooler's language. When you offer an incentive or reward, you are speaking their language and you actually make yourself "cool" by doing so!

Would you work for free? Not probable. Do you like surprises? Probable. Do you like getting something extra because you are being peaceful, happy, cooperative, and joyous at your work? Very probable! If you are asked to do something that makes you think, "I'm not sure I want to do that" in your head, would you do it more willingly for a bonus check? It is the same with middle school students!

Here is another view on parent to middle school student persuasion: Conducting family time or any other situation that says, "I'm not sure I want to do that" in a middle schooler's mind with a tangible reward makes things easier for all those involved. You get what you want. Your child gets something he or she has been wanting. It is a win-win situation and no one is upset, mad, or frustrated. It is just easier, calmer, and smoother. It is peaceful, happy, cooperative, and joyous. Yes, eventually, your child will grow up to have the wisdom that comes from age and experience, and will appreciate family time for the non-tangible rewards it offers—love, connectedness, belonging, caring, and togetherness. For now, rewards, bribery, and persuasion are key elements to create family harmony.

Create a Year-long Plan

Businesses do this. Sales people do this. CEOs do this. Teachers do this. Why not students?

Teachers have thick curriculum guides, which tell them what to teach kids in 180 days. Those 180 days are equal to thirty-six weeks, which are traditionally divided into four parts or quarters. Each quarter lasts nine weeks or forty-five days. Teachers decide how to separate the curriculum into four parts and teach one part each nine weeks. Then, teachers create plans for each week to cover the curriculum for that quarter. Influences such as needed and available materials, holidays, guest speaker schedule, professional days, teacher work days, coordination with other subject teachers, district requirements, and timing for projects are all part of the thought process to create the year-long plan.

Likewise, students can create their own year-long plans. These help eliminate overwhelming feelings since they will see the year reduced to smaller chunks of time. Usually, at the beginning of the year, teachers give students a synopsis of their year-long plans, which include what will be taught each quarter. Students can create their plans based upon the teachers' plans. The students' plans help them to see the logical progression of the curriculum since they add the teachers' curriculum for each quarter to their own plans. It is very motivating to enter holidays, days off of school, breaks, friends' birthdays, school special events such as football games and pep rallies, personal events such as family trips and basketball try outs, among other things. How about reviewing your child's year-long plan together and include dates for rewards of goals achieved and/or mini breaks? As the year progresses, additional events, rewards, and studies are added. Student year-long plans provide two main services: (1) academic motivation for the entire school year; and (2) self-scheduling opportunity, since they can clearly see how much time is available before projects are due and avoid time crunches with team practices, for example.

Hopefully, your child's school provides student agendas. These are excellent to maintain daily homework, activities, and events. Student agendas usually include school rules, motivational quotes, organization ideas, and hall pass pages. While school agendas are extremely valuable for tracking day to day homework, the year-long plan is broader in its scope. I suggest getting a large wall calendar of the entire year or a large desk calendar to create your child's year-long plan. What does your child prefer?

~

Talk to Others

I still vividly remember talking to my sister's friend who attended the same high school I was about to start. She discussed the dances, homework, teachers, activities, fun, lunchroom, lockers, uniforms, and so on. It was such a relief to talk to her! I reviewed that conversation all summer long.

Student to student conversation is quite honest and can be reassuring. Be choosy who your child questions about the middle school experience to ensure confidence will be the end result for your child. Most middle school students love to tell about their school experiences. There is much to tell! I have worked at three middle schools and they all have their own personalities, activities, and methods of doing things. If you can find (again, ask the principal or receptionist) a current or former student from the middle school your child will be attending, this can alleviate many concerns.

~

Write a Letter

As silly as this sounds, kids love receiving letters they wrote to themselves at a later date especially if they have forgotten about them. Have your middle school student write a letter at the beginning of the summer about middle school concerns, feelings, and questions, as well as the excitement, the wonderings, and the thrills! Assure your child you will not read the letter unless you have permission.

Seal the envelope and save it for a much later time when you feel it would be effective for your child to read it. As a teacher, I gave them back out at the end of the school year. The surprised looks on their faces were precious when reading the letters in May. Students laughed at what they wrote realizing their concerns never materialized. They glowed with personal acknowledgement that they made it through the year. Maturity occurred right then and there on the spot, knowing just how far they had come since August!

You decide the best time to return your child's letter or to send your child's letter in the mail. If your child is struggling during the year, perhaps send it earlier than the end of the school year. Use this letter as a way to give confidence to your child.

You can participate in this as well. Write a letter to your son or daughter at the beginning of school. Give the letter when you believe best. Can you get other family members, such as aunts, uncles, cousins, and grandparents, to participate with letter writing? Since each year of middle school is so different from the others, surprise letter writing can be done annually.

In addition, there are many reasons to write multiple letters to your child within a school year. After a particularly rough time send a supportive letter, after a successful time send a celebratory letter, or send a "just because" letter anytime!

> "Hmmmmm...this is a really good idea because some things can't always be stated easily by family members. Sometimes writing stuff down is better. Also, these letters could be put into a memory file or box for later as great mementos of this age. Thanks! I like this one a lot!"

Plan Future Events

As the first day of school approaches, nervousness usually increases. Potential problems seep into the psyche and mind games begin. For the sanity of both parents and students, plan a favorite activity a week or two after the first day of school. The psychology behind this suggestion is that the new-to-middle-school-student will think, "I will survive the first day of middle school because I'm going on the camping trip at the end of the week." Or, "I will live through the first week of school to have my slumber party that Friday night."

Or, "I can do this. I will live to shop for that dress Mom promised me." Just about anything is survivable if there is a desired planned activity to look forward to in the near future. It does make things better for everyone. Really!

~

Be Busy

If you or your child is especially anxious about middle school, be extra busy the weeks and days before the first day of school. Transpose nervous energy into a house project (paint the house, plant the garden, build the deck), a camping trip, a family vacation, or multiple activities during the day, such as swimming in the AM, tennis playing in the PM, and movie watching in the evening. Positive TV, electronic games, and movies are a great way to alleviate anxiety, as they serve as an escape from reality for a short period of time.

~

Recognize "Survivors"

You are not alone! All over the world there are millions of people doing things for the first time. It is a wonderful part of life. With this perspective, starting middle school is so exciting! Here are some firsts to consider:

First…

- day in kindergarten, elementary, middle, high school, or college

- time as starting as quarterback, soccer score, hole in one, or touchdown

- time bicycle riding without training wheels or car driving experience

- job, sale, or marketing presentation

- child birthing experience, feeding of solid foods, or changing a diaper
- sky diving experience, travel to foreign country, or public speaking
- day in boot camp, time making a fire, or time camping
- loose tooth, piano recital, or staying home alone
- time baking cookies without assistance
- crush, flirt, phone call, kiss, or date

The list goes on and on! The truth is that "firsts" offer humans so much more in comparison to repeatedly experiencing what is familiar. Everyone goes through "first time" experiences hundreds of times throughout life. It is an important part of life! It is now your opportunity and your child's opportunity to experience it for middle school. Remind him of his other firsts. This will not be the last of her first experiences and having *this* first with middle school will give your middle schooler confidence for the rest of her firsts!

Recognize Past Achievements

What has happened already that went well? What were those milestones of achievement, of success, of gaining personal pride? We all have them and with a personal review, these can be comforting to a student about to embark on a new adventure.

Every kid has achievements no matter how insignificant or significant. Maybe walking into kindergarten on one's own two feet was a really great feat. Do you know how many kids are carried, walk in crying, or can barely be convinced to release their grips from their parents' legs? If your child walked into kindergarten with a calm demeanor, this was an achievement! List any achievements, together preferably, then review them, recognize them, remember them, honor them, and celebrate them! No achievement is too small to feel the sense of accomplishment that the memory offers.

Perhaps, your shy child made one friend during an entire year, which may have been a tremendous feat. Your child figured out how to use scissors. Your child's handwriting improved. Your child learned to enjoy a certain food. Your child remained calm when taking turns being line leader or waiting to talk to the teacher.

Of course, celebrate the bigger achievements too. He learned how to dive. She recited a poem at a PTA meeting. He packed his own book bag the night before school, gathered organizational skills, remembered to care for the family pet, completed the laundry process, discovered ability to ride a bike, assisted landscaping the backyard willingly, or made supper for the first time without help. Was there an instrument recital to celebrate? Is there a sports game to remember? Was there a family move to a new location that was handled well? Is there a competition performance to honor?

Celebrate all achievements of the past with the focus on middle school, which is the next opportunity for learning, achieving, and celebrating! Since your child is capable of so many things (listed on the sheet you made together) she can now walk confidently into middle school, carry out all the things asked, positively interact with others using the inner guide (feelings) to handle the interactions, make friends, relate to teachers, navigate the hallways, mind the school procedures, manage time, complete homework punctually, and more. When it is time to focus on the next opportunity for learning, achieving, and celebrating (high school), you can make a list of middle school achievements to calm pre-high school jitters!

~

Focus on What The School Offers

People love discussing which schools are better than others, what kind of students attend which schools, which schools have good reputations, and.... Well, the truth is that every middle school has pros and cons. There are really, really good teachers at every school. There are really, really smart students at every school. There are really, really good aspects to every school.

Schools located in affluent areas are not always better. "Rich" schools have their own set of issues too. Low-economic schools receive much government financial support, which affords opportunity for lower student to teacher ratios, provides after school programs, funds field trips easier, finances innovative ideas, repairs building issues quicker, and offers funds for extras such as end of year school celebrations.

Focus on what your child's school has to offer. Take advantage of those things. Be proud of the school. Talk in the community about the wonderful things the school is providing for your child. Take an active role to help the school achieve even greater success. Recognize that every middle school has pros and cons, and focus on what is good with yours.

If there are issues or problems with your child's school, identify the cause, then target the solution and go for it. Which feels better? The problem or the solution? Easy answer for that question! All perceived negative situations are only opportunities waiting to happen, but it does depend on the focus. Know of parents who like to talk and talk about school problems? Guide them to a solution and strongly encourage them to take action. Both you and they will feel relieved. No more negative talk, but talk of changes and talk of improvements!

Focus on how your child's teachers try really hard to make things go smoothly and enjoyable. Notice every calculated step because teachers spend much time preparing for a good day or a fascinating lesson or a positive event. Focus on the effort the teachers and others in the building did to prepare the school building for children. What about the hallway decorations? The potted plants in the office? The clean (or reasonably clean – hey, it is middle school!) floors? What about the display of student work? Can you see evidence of honoring those who do well? How about the sofa or other lounging furniture in the library? There is always something positive to focus upon in each school. Find it. Focus on it. Make it a big deal and watch the positive vibes overflow into all the areas of the school.

~

Prepare For Thanking Teachers, Administrators, and Other School Staff

> "Thanking teachers, administrators, and other school staff? What does this have to do with getting ready for a school year and providing a smooth transition to middle school?? And what about those who don't want to do this or can't afford teacher gift giving?"

I do acknowledge that some parents do not want to or are not able to thank teachers, administration, and/or support staff with a physical gift. I also acknowledge that some schools do not even allow this. No matter your situation, please read this section as it provides you with a new perspective on this subject and others. Despite whatever choice you decide about thanking the employees at your child's school, the best gift of all to every teacher, administration, and support staff person is providing a polite, motivated-for-success child each day.

If you *do* plan to provide teachers, administration, and/or support staff tangible gift, then when the holiday season or the end of the year comes, you will thank me for putting this topic in the book. And yes, I am putting it in "the before school starts section" because it is a decision you can make now. Most middle school students enjoy giving gifts, and they probably will have more teachers, administrators, support staff, and friends than they did in elementary school. Why not start making holiday gifts or budget the money now?

Fast forward four months to the holiday season, which will come faster than you think. You really, really like your child's teachers and want to do something special for each one. What to do…what to do? Now that your child is in middle school, there could be six or more teachers. That is a lot of expense. So, you think about going with the holiday coffee cup with a fat Santa and a reindeer on it filled with strawberry hard candies…or peppermint candies…or caramel candies. Please, and I feel confident to speak on behalf of the thousands of teachers out there, no more coffee cups stuffed with candy!

In an article Neena Samuel wrote called, "13 Things Your Child's Teacher Won't Tell You,"[2] Ms. Samuel reveals a few things teachers would love to tell parents, but don't feel comfortable expressing. She writes, "Please, no more mugs, frames, or stuffed animals. A gift card to Starbucks or Staples would be more than enough. A thank-you note: even better."

OK, it is not that I or other teachers did not appreciate the generosity and gifts given over the years. But after seventeen years of teaching, do you know how many coffee mugs I received? And, I don't even drink coffee! Do parents want fat, jittery teachers with their children? I used the coffee cups to hold pencils, markers, paper clips, rubber bands, and other miscellaneous mysterious items that inevitably ended up on my teacher desk. Yes, teachers are thankful for these cups, but enough is enough!

What do teachers really want? Well, to start this discussion (and please hold on till the end because there is a point!), we will need to first look at the fact that teachers' roles in society are extremely important, yet the monetary compensation is inadequate.

> "But, many argue that teachers have much vacation time throughout the year so the salary is in proportion to time actually teaching. Isn't the salary compensation appropriate for working 180 days out of 365 days?"

It is really 190 days a year, but still, even in states where teachers are paid "well," the salary is not in proportion to the time spent outside of work after hours correcting papers, preparing lessons plans, gathering lesson supplies, participating in continuing education courses (often at personal expense), attending evening PTA meetings, tutoring students, mentoring afterschool clubs, talking to parents on the phone, answering parent emails late at night, creating weekly newsletters, updating online parent and student resources, and using personal funds for classroom supplies.

Teachers do have summer vacation—a.k.a. Sanity Finding Time. There are those long breaks during holidays too. Really? Teachers spend most holidays correcting papers and preparing lessons. A teacher's summer time is spent in continuing education or miscellaneous training and at least two week's preparation prior to the start of the next academic school year. Subtract all those time-consuming events from the summer and there might be two to three weeks remaining.

> "Well, all that information sounded pretty negative about the teaching career. Where's the upside about it since this is a positive book, right? And, what does this have to do with showing appreciation or thankfulness at holiday times?"

OK. Why have I included all this information? To put all into perspective for anyone needing to see a more complete picture of the teachers' challenging working environment. Here is the real scoop on teacher gifts, and it probably will be different than you think! First, what gift teachers want most is a healthy working relationship with parents all year long. What gift teachers want most is a classroom full of polite, eager-to-learn students. What gift teachers want most is to be able to do their job—teach. Just being a supportive parent and sending a well-mannered student ready to learn to school each day is the best present of all. Beyond this, gift certificates are incredibly appreciated. Teachers spend an immense amount of personal money at stores offering edible and tangible reward/prize items and teacher supplies. Gift certificates to these places are much appreciated. In this way, teacher gifts help teachers help your child. If teacher gifts help teachers help your child, isn't that helping you too?

Gift certificates to "luxury" places are treasured gifts for a whole different reason. Pedicures, manicures, massages, or any other spa type service are not only luxuries, but healthy. Teachers spend most of the time on their feet. Pedicures are so soothing and stimulate the nerve endings on the bottom of feet, which stimulate the entire body to health! It is like giving a loving massage to every internal organ. Manicures are beneficial because teacher hands get quite dry due to handling so much paper, which removes moisture from hands. Massages release stress, tension, and toxins stored in tense teacher muscles. Spa treatments return stable and balanced psyches to exhausted teachers. Can you think of other ideas to improve the health of your child's teachers? Organic fruit baskets, movie tickets, and restaurant gift certificates are other suggestions. Teacher gifts help teachers stay healthy and remain with your child in the classroom.

Collecting monies from many parents to provide ongoing gifts, "large" gifts, or special lunches are all deeply cherished. How about a year's subscription to a fitness club such as a racquetball club, tennis club, or swimming club? How about flower of the month gifts? Chocolate, coffee, wine, book, or fruit of the month gifts? If your town is touristy, how about a ticket to be a tourist in your own town? Periodic special lunches are so appreciated. All these teacher gifts make teachers feel valued, which helps teachers value your child. If teachers feel valued by your efforts, which make them feel appreciation toward your child, would that make your child express appreciation toward you? Would that appreciation coming from your child make you feel appreciation toward your child's teachers all over again? That is a circle of appreciation going round and round!

Are you crafty? There are many gifts to make that are low cost and quite useful to school employees. Suggestions are: aprons (for messy lessons), lanyards (for school identification badges or glasses), back and seat cushions (for those hard plastic chairs), split tennis balls (for the bottom of all student chairs legs and desk legs – for much quieter rooms), a series of pockets (for all the "stuff" teachers have that needs storing), decorated planters for plants (for the front office too), overhead projector wraps (for storing the special pens and markers used on the equipment), decorated boxes/shelving (for all the papers teachers "collect"), pointers (for fun teaching - made of dowel rods, stuffing, and gardening gloves), and humorous t-shirts (for humor in the classroom – made with a white undershirt with fabric paint). There are so many other ideas for fun and pretty low cost gifts!

How about purchasing sports, piano recital, or talent show tickets to your child's event for the teachers? You support your child with teacher attendance and you have given nice teacher gifts. Now, that's another win-win situation! Teachers who attend your child's events outside of school gain a new perspective of your child. Do you see how reciprocal teacher gifts are for you and your child? When you give to them, you are really giving a gift to your child, which is really giving a gift to yourself!

> "Yeah. I do see your point. Instead of dreading or feeling obligated to give teachers, administrators, or other school support staff gifts, I can see the benefit for my child and me. I *do* want my child to interact with healthy and happy people. I think I really understand now."

Good. I do have another point for this topic! Second, it can be embarrassing for middle school kids to carry and deliver six to ten teacher gifts. Many middle school students do not have the social maturity to give gifts and handle that kind of personal conversation with teachers. I have seen anguish on the faces of kids whose parents told them to deliver the gifts. They did it as fast as they could and felt lucky if the teachers were absent so they could deposit gifts on desks in solitude. Please ask how your child feels regarding gift delivery. If uncomfortable, take the gifts to the school yourself after obtaining a building pass. The front office personnel can handle the gift distribution too.

No matter what gift you decide upon, I recommend you start planning during the summer. If you are not able to afford gifts, it is just fine, and is really important that you feel OK with this. Focus on prosperity for yourself and send your nice, polite, well-mannered, ready-to-learn child to school. That is the best gift every day!

Save or Budget For School Extras

There will be many miscellaneous monetary "opportunities" when your child will need, want, or ask you for money throughout the year. I suggest putting some money aside for these things now so that you have the money when needed, because these incidentals add up quickly. Most schools supplement their budgets by conducting many fundraisers for school extras, such as end of year celebrations, graduation dinners and awards, or school dances. If there is a needy family or tragic event in the community, a special fundraiser will most likely be organized too. So, expect to be offered the "opportunity" to buy boxes of fruit, gift wrapping supplies, cookie mixes, pizza mixes, and seasonal items from catalogues, in addition to school clothing, school memorabilia, raffle tickets, and candy bars. Other school activities that require funds from parents may include a yearbook; school spirit t-shirts; school bumper stickers; extra school supplies like garment bags; instruments; sports registration fees; sports uniforms or musical performance outfits; pizza, candy, and drinks at school dances; and field trips. At the middle school level, field trips may take on a whole new meaning with multiple day and overnight excursions to places farther from home. This means higher costs, perhaps several hundred dollars and more. Yes, budgeting or saving money now for school extras is highly recommended!

Delay Purchasing Beginning of Year School Supplies

Do not purchase all the items on a school supply list before school starts.

> "Um…why? I want to get it done and shop before everyone else so that I can purchase all the items on the list. I hate it when the stores run out! It is usually one item and then I have to remember to get it later. I like one-stop shopping."

Purchase the necessary items—loose leaf paper, pens, pencils, and so on. The lists are made at the end of the previous year by the existing teachers when teachers are stressed out, tired, and hurried. Many things can change over the summer, primarily faculty. Each teacher does things differently and a newly hired teacher may want different school supplies. Remember all the things teachers do over the summer during their "vacation" time? Teachers, once relieved of the stress, may get "ah-ha!" moments and alter how they conduct their classrooms, which may mean different school supplies.

I have seen it happen year after year. The list is loaded with many items. Parents purchase the entire list and then are frustrated with excess and/or unnecessary supplies. Wait until your child sees all teachers and receives the course syllabus for each class with the required supplies. Send your child to school with the basics like pencils, paper, pencil box, and glue, but wait on the specific school supplies. Teachers give grace periods for adjustment to the new school year. Obtaining all school supplies is part of this adjustment period. You will be able to shop in peace as you won't have the masses of people in the school supply aisle *before* school starts! By this time, stores have restocked their shelves abundant with glue, paper, folders, binders, and pencils.

If you just do not want to wait until after school has started, another option is to obtain email confirmation ahead of the start of school regarding school supplies. Most teachers answer emails one to two weeks prior to the start of school.

Set Goals with Tangible Rewards

What motivates you in life? In your work life? What makes you want to do something? Why do you complete some projects with gusto? Would you work for free? Would you accomplish an assigned task well if there was no reward or benefit for you? In the business world, a job well done gets rewarded. A job not so well done receives an action plan for improvement. Your child does not want to work for free. Your child likes rewards. School is the job.

I recognize the two divergent thoughts on the subject of rewarding students. Education is fun. Gaining knowledge is a wonderful feeling.

But, would you want to work just for fun or for a wonderful feeling? Most middle school students do not pay much attention to their intrinsic motivation. It is all about the extrinsic. What is in it for me? What do I get?

No matter what side of the debate you are on, please consider just how much easier you will make things for all those involved if you provide some type of reward for a job well done for your child, which is more reflective of the "real world." These incentives are best if they are established before school starts and established *with* your child. He then will have ownership of the goal setting and reward system. By doing this, you are putting both you and your child on the same team. Resistance is just about eliminated. Motivation spikes to an all-time high. You set your child up for success! Can you already feel the smiles, agreement, and happiness in your house day after day?

Tangible rewards really work well with the middle school aged child. If she can hold it (new shoes), feel it (new clothing), experience it (movie), play with it (basketball), and/or taste it (favorite meal), the reward is all the more effective and motivating. The five senses play a significant role in rewards with middle school students.

Possible reward ideas are to arrange for a special event, such as a boating trip with a friend, camping trip, shopping trip, pizza party with friends, pottery painting, manicures, pedicures, massages, or a beauty salon trip. Some ideas like traveling to a new place can be rewarding and educational at the same time. An A in history class might deserve a trip to Fort Sumter, SC, where the Civil War started, or to Gettysburg, PA, where Abraham Lincoln's Emancipation Proclamation was first spoken. An A in science might deserve a trip to the Monterey Bay Aquarium in Monterey, CA. Would New York City, Chicago, or San Francisco be motivating to a middle schooler? You bet!

Other less costly ideas are spending time with you or friends, swimming at the pool, staying up later than usual, making a favorite meal, arranging for a special tour of a local college or business, playing sports, or painting nails. Ask your middle schooler what he would like. Your middle school child will not have any trouble telling you what he would like for a reward!

Frequency of reward? This is a bit tricky because your child's motivation and attention span will determine the frequency. How often or how long can your child go without a reward? Most middle school students need regular and frequent rewards. Perhaps building up to a large end of year reward such as a trip to Massachusetts's Naismith Memorial Basketball Hall of Fame with little rewards at each interim progress report would work well. Knowing your child, your child's motivation level, and your child's past academic record will greatly assist in the creation of a goal and reward system.

"Obtainability" is key to the success of the plan. Obtainable rewards are as important as obtainable goals. If your child is not a straight A student, then all B's or all C's might be obtainable. The point is to create motivation to stretch your child to new heights. Plan a reward that you know you can deliver, meaning rewards must be obtainable for you to provide. Promising a trip to Niagara Falls when you live in New Mexico on a tight budget might not be obtainable. The goals and rewards must be able to be obtainable for both of you.

Post the plan in highly visible areas for your child. It could be part of your child's monthly calendar on a desk or wall. Remember, you know your child best. Keep it simple for those who get overwhelmed easily. Add more if it is meaningless. Create the plan to include anything positive, such as helping around the house (e.g., cleaning her bedroom every Saturday), keeping schoolwork pleasant (e.g., homework is complete before 8 PM), or speaking in a friendly voice (e.g., positive peer interactions). The posted plan *must* contain *only* positively stated goals.

Simplified example:

Goal:	Mid-Term	Yes/ No	End of Quarter	Yes/ No	Reward
All B's or above	Mid-October		Early November		Pizza Party with three friends
All B+'s or above	Early January		Early February		Ice Hockey Game with one friend
All A's or above	Mid-March		Early April		New Baseball Glove
All A+'s	Early May		June 6th!		Trip to San Francisco!

"What if my child doesn't make the goal for the mid-term progress report, but does make the goal by the end of the quarter?"

The important part of goal setting is to reach the goals, keep motivation high, and achieve academic and personal success. You can decide what do to by observing your child. Did he have a hard time starting school, but then through great effort found a method to achieve? Did she slack off until the end, but still made the goal? In scenario one, I would suggest amending the reward to something similar, but not the exact pre-determined reward, such as having only two friends with a pizza party. In scenario two, I would suggest amending the whole plan and using smaller increments of time with smaller, but more often, rewards for achieving the desired goal. This child needs help with being a consistent student and respecting the daily lessons, not just the ones at the end of the quarter.

Visualize

Visualize a good experience for yourself and your child and encourage your child to do this over the summer as well. See your child walking confidently into the building and returning with smiles every day. Visualize your child becoming good friends with many, developing positive acquaintances with the rest, and getting along with the largest, apparently toughest child. Spend time soaking up the pleasure you will receive in parent-teacher conferences as the teachers talk about your child's awesomeness. (This would be enhanced if you see your child as awesome too. If you do not see your child as awesome, now would be a great time to start visualizing this.) Ponder the positive vibes at award ceremonies as your child receives recognition for success. Smile from the vision of your child taking leadership roles in the school, accepting privileges (such as running the AV equipment for morning news program) for his responsibility and trustworthiness, and collecting positive vibes as he is well known throughout the school by administrators, teachers, and support staff. There are always kids who stick out and are known throughout the entire school for just being plain ol' awesome. Why not your kid?

Believe enough in your visualizations that they do come true and become your reality. Feel them! Expect them! Expect: good things, that all is well, and that your child will listen to her internal wisdom with every situation. Expect: that your child will enjoy his middle school experience and that every person, assignment, interaction, and moment will be for his positive human being progression. Visualize it now. Feel it now. Expect it now.

Have your child visualize positively handling the varied interactions with the many different personality types that he will encounter in middle school. Have your child feel the success pumping through his blood as he receives that first good grade from a test or project that he created from appropriate effort. Can your child envision the fun to be had in the cafeteria? With friends in the hallways? With teachers in classrooms? With administrators at school functions?

> "I see how visualizing is a great tool for me, as the parent, and for my child. Visualizing seems fun because of all the possibilities that exist in visualization."

Yes, visualizing is where the possibilities exist! Visualizing is what makes one *aware* of the possibilities and helps narrow down which possibilities to pursue. Visualizing is essential to *any* creation! Can anything be done without the ideas popping in one's head first? Nope. Human beings visualize first, and then take action. Even if it is a split second of a vision, this is still the order in which ANYTHING is created, produced, or accomplished. Visualization becomes a wonderful experience, especially when the images are coupled with positive feelings—then they are enhanced! The feelings really assist with making the visualizations reality.

Here is an example of visualization: See your child at the school lockers getting books for the next few classes. There are kids everywhere laughing, joking, smiling, and having fun while conducting their book exchanges. You can hear, "Oops!" or "Can you get that for me?" or "I'm sorry," as books fall by mistake. The noise level is pleasantly loud because it is the joyful middle school noise! Your child shuts the locker door and walks confidently toward the next classroom destination. The hallway is bright and cheerful. You continue to see your child smiling and laughing while absorbing the experience. You hear someone compliment your child's outfit. Feel the contentment of being positively recognized by a peer. As the group heads to the next classroom, feel the intense joy of belonging that your child feels. Feel the "deep in the stomach" silliness as someone retells a story of another saying or doing something humorous in yesterday's class. Feel the slight elbow bumping from the student nearby. Hear the shoe squeaks echoing down the long hallway. Smell the stale book smell wafting up from the books in your child's arms. It's all good… very good.

> "And while I am imaging such a delightful middle school scenario, just how does that make it a reality?"

You bring it toward you to be included in your life like a fisherman focuses as he reels in his catch, like deciding which of the massive selection of TV channels to watch, like cropping and color editing a photo so that it matches how one wants it to look, like adjusting one's voice to bring forth the best sound, like practicing a synchronized swimming routine to perfection, like tuning a piano, or like practicing partner dance steps. Visualizing is focusing on a desired outcome with strong intent. Visualizing what you want and feeling good about it makes both the desired situation and you a match! You and the scenario are in sync. You vibrate at the same level. You unite with the energy of the visualization.

"You unite with the energy of the visualization?? What does that mean?"

Yeah, I figured that last sentence might catch your attention! It is pretty simply what I mean. If you match your pleasant thoughts (visualizations) with your positive emotions (vibes, energy, vibrations), then you can bring forth, attract to you, pull into your life, or create the scenario in your life. It just happens! This does require that you forget about how it will happen and trust that life will bring it to you. Just go with the pleasant thoughts and positive emotions.

Here is another explanation: Have you ever experienced feeling noticeably different because someone entered a room in which you were sitting? Why? Humans are made of trillions of cells. Each cell is made of particles of energy called atoms. Atoms are tiny "balls" of energy. Even these balls of energy can be further reduced in size, but they are still all energy! So, each cell is a basic unit of energy. This energy collectively radiates out from our bodies and searches for matches. Ever just "click" with another person instantly? Ever get "weird vibes" from someone? Ever get a "gut feeling" that someone is lying to you? Ever have someone you just love hanging out with you? The collective energy radiating out from our bodies is why hugs can feel great! When your collective body energy finds matches, you feel connected, good, and peaceful. When it finds energy that does not match, you feel unnerved, uneasy, and disconnected. So when a person enters a room in which you were sitting, it will either feel good or uneasy depending upon your vibrational match to the person.

This collective energy radiating out from your body also works well with thoughts and sources of information too. I limit my TV watching, especially the news. I am very picky about what I watch on TV, view on the Internet, read from a reading source, and hear from another because my collective energy serves as a perfect guide for me to determine what feels good to me and what does not feel good to me. Feeling good is my top priority! When you visualize what you really want out of life and you become an energetic match to it (your positive emotions), it feels good…naw…it feels great! Maintain this energetic level and you will attract what you have been visualizing or focusing. Your thoughts hold this energetic power!

Ever get a case of the "negative nellies"? Nothing is going as planned and negative thinking abounds. How does your body feel? Slow? Tired? Weighted? When I get stuck in this rut, I usually have to take a nap because it is tiring to think negatively. What happens, then, when some positive diversion (higher energetic level) comes along (because you focused on wanting to feel better) like a good friend, a positive phone call, a faithful pet, an unexpected gift, or a beautiful nature scene such as puffy clouds? How does your body feel then? Energized? Fresher? Lighter? Each and every single cell in your body becomes more energetic. You can *feel* the difference! People will ask, "Do you feel better now?" Well, yes, you do because you are vibrating at an increased level and it does feel better!

Have you ever come home from a long day at work tired and exhausted? Have you ever been this way and just want to rest for the entire evening? Have you ever had your plans diverted because of some inspiration, fun, or good feeling distraction such as the movie you have been waiting for is now playing, or your best friend just told you that there are wonderful sales at the mall? Suddenly, you have energy! You change your evening plans and spend a great time at the mall. What made the difference? The focus shifted from the negative to the positive and your body responded as a perfect match to your visualization of purchasing something special. Your thoughts, visualizations, and feelings are ways to stir up your energy to be a match to the greatness of life! So utilizing the visualization tool before middle school starts is extremely useful. Take time to visualize the best experience you can image for your child and then add positive emotions. You will be amazed just what you see!

"I used to do this as a kid! It's sorta like day dreaming. It was fun to visualize what I really wanted to happen. The more I thought about it, the more I became excited about what I was day dreaming about. It was fun!"

Yes, daydreaming is a healthy activity! One more thing can be added to this suggestion of visualization: honor the visualizations with a quiet place and maybe even a recording of the visions, as in a journal, on a story line, a bulletin board, or a bathroom mirror. Journaling visualizations for your child can be as easy as writing a sentence or two, writing a page or two, or drawing an image or two! A story line is putting the images on a string in some kind of order. Hang yarn from one wall to another and add your written or drawn visualizations. Put them on a bulletin board or a bathroom mirror or a bedroom wall or the bedroom ceiling or….

Plan Your Child's Niche

Depending on your child's interests, can your child soak up the positive vibes of what it is going to be like to be the art teacher's apprentice? The computer teacher's aide? The audio-visual technician? The school decorator? The student public relations speaker? The school's student representative at the major's inauguration? The student whom all staff call upon for help? Prior to starting middle school, ponder your child's skills and how these skills can be utilized in a middle school setting. Ponder your child's niche, place, function, or forte.

There was a student in one of the middle schools I taught at who knew more about computers than any other student. Because he was polite, academic, and quick to fix computer issues, he often was called for assistance. Everyone knew him in the school, everyone respected him, and everyone cried the day he graduated from middle school! This student went on to high school and did the same for those teachers too. In addition, he conducted a computer repair business in his neighborhood. From the time this esteemed student, who wowed us with his ability to talk to teachers confidently and to fix computers accurately, walked into sixth grade and walked out of eighth grade, he had a wonderful, awesome, successful, and thrilling middle school experience.

What talent does your child have that could assist the teachers, administrators, and school? Is your child talented in art? She could assist teachers with room displays, hallway displays, murals, and banners. Is your child talented with interior design? He could assist making the school building bright and cheerful. Is your child talented with music? He could assist the band director with the many, many programs and parent nights, orchestrating music for these school functions. Is your child talented with public speaking? There are many opportunities that teachers would LOVE to use this talent. Is your child talented with cooking or baking? Do I even have to elaborate on this one? How can your child fit in, fill a need, constructively use talents, and demonstrate her unique path (a.k.a. interests) in the school? Many, many opportunities abound! Visualize it! Feel it! Expect it! Great schools are filled with student-led activities.

Do you realize just how many community people and companies would jump at the chance to help a student with a vision? For instance, if your child loves plants and the outdoors and created landscaping plans for the middle school, it would not take very long to obtain donations in the form of time, resources, and machinery from the community. Plants, shrubs, flowers, trees, dirt, concrete, mulch, stones, and so on, almost would appear out of thin air! Why? The community is driven by an innate desire to assist the young. People love to "show their stuff." It is great public relations and advertising for their companies. It also just makes people feel good to help others. It is a really positive feeling to be part of something big in one's community, especially with something that will last for years to come. Such a landscaping project would fit into this category.

"I remember feeling so awesome when I was helpful to my teachers in school. It was fun reversing roles when I could assist *them*. It was the first time I really felt part of something bigger than me. I want that for my child!"

Yes, it does feel good to know one's place and to utilize talents in positive ways. Good schools will allow this kind of student leadership readily. What is your child's niche?

~

So as promised, I've given you many practical ideas and suggestions to pre-paving your middle school child's way through these years. I hope they have sparked great ideas and motivation in you. There are many options to create wonderful, awesome, successful, and thrilling experiences! Won't it be a really great feeling to do many of these ideas and see the incredible results from your efforts? What does this feel like? Can you visualize your son or daughter achieving success right in front of you? Can you hear the excitement in his voice about school? Can you hear, "Mom, I got an A on my math test! See??" Can you smell the pizza you have ordered for a reward for your daughter and her friends? Can you now experience the growing sense of pride and joy swelling up inside of you, almost to the point of tears? Now, that is pre-paving your child's way for middle school success!

But, here's one more very important strategy for handling pre-school jitters.

~

Parents and Students, Relax!

At some point prior to the start of school, you and your child just need to relax. By this, I mean in *addition* to physically relaxing. Of course, lounging by the pool, sleeping in, getting together with friends, and snuggling with a good book are all terrific ways to physically relax. But I want to convey a definition of relax at a deeper level… at the soul level.

This is that level when you know and feel "all is well," "I'll be able to handle everything," and "it's all perfect just the way it is." Can you relax to the point knowing that life is a safe experience? That life supports you, not tests you? That the goal of life is to have fun, joy, and happiness? That life is for you, not against you? Relaxing at this level is true relaxation. And, why not? Have you not prepared yourself and your child for a successful year? If you can feel this level of relaxation, you allow positive things, people, events, and situations to come to you.

> "Are you kidding here? Visualization…relaxation…believing that life will be great by doing these things? Are you proposing that it can be this easy? Isn't this a bit too much fluff? Life can be hard and it takes true grit to make one's way in life, including in middle school."

Not a believer that life supports you and that life is on your side? Well, keep reading and by the end of this book, I am pretty sure you will understand how wonderful, awesome, successful, and thrilling life can be for you, the parent, and for your child. Good things can happen with a focus on what you want in life. Sounds pretty simple, huh? I will elaborate on this concept and the single most important key to wonderful, awesome, successful, and thrilling middle school experiences in the next section. Yes, these can positively affect your child's experience in middle school, as well as all other areas too!

FIVE

The Single Most Important Key to A Wonderful, Awesome, Successful, and Thrilling Middle School Experience

Don't you just get annoyed when authors write such titles as the one above? It makes one wonder just what is that single most important key to ______ (you fill in the blank). Do I have that single most important key? Am I doing it? What? What IS it? I just gotta know! It always seemed that the single most important key to whatever was always something I did not like to eat (as with diets), want to do (as with exercise routines), or was out of my reach (as with seminars on the other side of the country). Many times, it was something to purchase, which I did not want to do either. Usually, the single most important key did not agree with me. My intentional attention grabbing title above is referring to something you already have, something you probably already do, and something you can do relatively easily.

"You're doing it to us! You're using the type of title just to get our attentions! I can jive pretty well with all the other ideas you have presented in this book so far, so I'm waiting patiently, but enough already… what is it??

Drum roll, please. The…single…most…important…key…to wonderful, awesome, successful, and thrilling middle school experiences is…a complete positive view of middle school. Yes. That's it…a complete positive view of middle school. OK, there is a bit more to it. An explanation is coming shortly, but is this something you already have? No need to spend any money. Is this something you probably already are doing? There is probably no need to make drastic changes. Is this something you can do relatively easily? Well, wait to answer this question. There is an aspect of having a positive view of middle school that makes it *super* effective.

If you have not been holding, believing, or expressing a complete positive view about middle school, then a true change of opinion about middle school years is so important for both you and your child. No matter when you start this, you can experience the positive effects right away. Learn to feel the wonderful difference of energy with positive thinking. Pre-pave the way for your child with any new situation at any time!

"Yeah, I've heard lots about positive thinking and how those people say it can bring about the good stuff of life. But really now…things happen in life. Just by thinking positively we can avoid those things?"

It is like you "rev" up your engine to a higher speed or vibration and you make yourself a match to what you really, really want out of life. So, yes, positive thinking does "rev" your engine to make it match to the good stuff of life! It can take some effort and time to switch to such an outlook on middle school or any aspect of life. So, in the process of becoming totally positive, things might happen that you would not prefer.

~

TIISG with Everything

Dr. Joe Vitale writes about TIISG in his book, *The Attractor Factor.*[3] What is TIISG? It is a way of looking for the good in any situation no matter how awful you think it is. What did I just write there… "no matter how awful you *think* it is"? Yup! It is that thinking issue again. You get what you focus on. TIISG stands for "Turn It Into Something Good." Whatever happens, whatever is currently in your life, whatever is bothering you right now, TIISG!

I have had quite difficult things happen in my life. For example, I have been divorced…twice. I learned a whole heck of a lot about myself, so I would not trade the experiences for anything. I TIISGed them!

Divorce was the apparent negative situation in my life that became opportunity through which I became awakened to new levels of understanding about life. I awoke spiritually, meaning I became aware that I am more a non-physical being than a physical being. I also became aware of the real definition and availability of wealth for everyone. Pretty cool, huh? I also really woke up to the power of my thoughts. I ignorantly focused on the past and what did not go smoothly in my first marriage, and well, that is what I got…again. So my second marriage mirrored my first marriage. I was quite bewildered when I discovered that I was in similar marriage. I asked over and over, "How did I do this? How did I end up here again?" The answer came to me in the books I started reading on how to obtain what I wanted out of life. A huge light bulb went off in my head when I realized that I had attracted into my life what had been my focus! Since then, I have paid much attention to my thoughts and feelings, making sure they are in alignment with where I want to go. It was matter of switching my focus from the past to the future. And, do you know what? Many awesome things started to happen…not all at once, but changes definitely occurred. My "book angels" directed me to sources of information. Pertinent people entered my life. Out of the ordinary events happened. Desires manifested. I am nowhere near done focusing, desiring, and changing my life—it is an enjoyable, on-going creation. I can report that I now am married to a really great guy who has the characteristics and traits I was determined (focused) to have in my life. I am so incredibly thankful for what I learned!

My power is in my thoughts. I focus on what I want and *then* take action. What else can I attract with my thoughts? Well…in addition to attracting my current, wonderful husband, I attracted a lifestyle that allows me time to act on my writing passion. So, I now I actually utilize the miscellaneous pieces of paper with jotted notes and ideas, which had been stuffed into a folder for at least fifteen years! I am also a stay-at-home mom and assist my family like never before.

So, there is my testimony for the power of positive thinking. I have lived it. I have brought incredible people, events, and information into my life through the focus of my thoughts and excitement for my desires. My life has "morphed" into something much better than it was. This really works! TIISG everything!

There is great power in *your* thoughts too. What do you want to attract? Your thoughts are like magnets. Be aware of what you are focusing on primarily and predominantly each day. Once you are aware of your thoughts, you can make the decision to alter them if you wish.

> "If positive thoughts create positive things to happen, how is it, then, that most people have a little bit of good and a little bit of bad in their lives?"

If the predominant thoughts are a little bit of good and a little bit of bad, then that is the focus and that is what they get. If one can only focus on desire, wish, prosperity, love, peace, happiness, and freedom, then those would be the only things to appear. A lot of people focus on both and get both.

It is not that people with successful lives do not see the negatives of life in order to obtain the good stuff. The good stuff and the negative stuff do exist. It is just that one who is concerned with the quality of one's thoughts will not belabor on anything negative. For example: you drive by a mangled car that has been in an accident. What do you do with this? Do not keep reviewing the scene in your mind, do not talk about the car accident to others, and do not then watch the news to get all the nitty-gritty details. Instead, notice the accident then think about safety. Think about how you are traveling well and enjoying the driving experience, notice the clouds in the sky, feel the thankfulness that your car is so comfortable, and appreciate the other drivers around you who are alert and aware of your car's presence. Soon, you will be on to another positive thought far away from the car accident scene. In this scenario, what are you attracting?

"Then, why is it that some people who are focused on health get sick?"

It depends on how they are focused on the topic of health. If the focus is on health because they are fearful of getting sick, then the focus is on getting sick. If the focus is on health because it is fun to be healthy and fun to exercise, then health is what they will get. Here is another example: If one has been focusing on obtaining more money for the bank account and wondering where it is because the balance is still perceived as too low, the focus is on the lack of the money flowing in. If one has been focusing on obtaining more money to flow in the bank account and is excited about what can be done with the money, the focus is on the money flowing in.

Giving Power to Your Focus

Apply the power of your thoughts to anything in life, including middle school. Here is a very simple process for doing just that:

1. Make two lists on separate sheets of paper: one of the negatives and one of positives before the experience actually happens. These lists are very important.

2. Focus on the items on the positive list first. How do they make you feel?

3. Write a feeling statement next to the positive statement. Use all five senses as they apply to experience the desire before it happens.

4. Add to the positive list as you think of new ones throughout the year. Always include the feeling statements.

5. Add comments of celebration to the posted positive list as the year progresses. "I made a new friend the second day of school." "I found my way perfectly today." "I am keeping my papers organized." These individual achievements really add up to success when put together. Celebrate all of them no matter how small.

6. Keep the positive list on the refrigerator, in a journal, on a bathroom mirror, or wherever you are going to see and have time to read the positive list regularly. This is very important. Personally, I use my bathroom mirror.

> "OK. As a parent, I understand the steps you listed here, but do you really think that boys are going to do all of this? Feeling statements? Really now? Aren't you being a little silly to expect males to contemplate *and* write about their feelings?"

Males may perceive the feeling statements as too feminine. However, the point is to experience the positive before the actual experience. Boys have five senses, too, right? Feelings are not just feminine traits that belong to girls. In all of us are both feminine and masculine energies. Males can be kind, considerate, and emotional. To ridicule or embarrass a male for exhibiting these traits is to deny what is already in him, what has been a part of him since birth. It is what he is made of, not what he gathered along life's way.

Females can be physical, assertive, and brash. To make a female feel uncomfortable about demonstrating these traits goes against what is already inside of her, for she was created that way. Is it wise to totally embrace all of our traits? Yes! Do we not need all of what we were given for certain situations? Yes! Are there some emergency situations that females are glad to have masculine energies? Yes! When a father cries at the birth of his child, are we not glad he has that capability? Yes!

Is it wise to use only part of a gift? No! If we have two speakers with a sound system, do we only use one of the speakers? Do we only use one of our two eyes? Do we only use one of our hands? We all have both feminine and masculine energy inside us. So when it comes to writing feeling statements, males do have the capabilities in them to write, express, and experience emotions. It is already who they are.

Not so sure about this? Just say something offensive to a male like, "Your team sucks," or "Your Momma," and you will see plenty of emotion displayed! Ask a male to talk about his girlfriend and you will get emotions. Feeling a desire before it happens is what makes this all SUPER effective! Feel the success! Feel the triumph! Feel the greatness now and it will bring about the change or desired outcome faster.

Example:

Positive	Feeling	Celebrations
I can't believe I am at the age for middle school!	Feels great, like my heart is pounding through my whole body! I want to jump up and down!	I made it through the first week of middle school! It was fun!!
I'll be making more friends.	It feels a bit nervous and exciting at the same time! Sounds like pizza, popcorn, and parties!	I met my friend, Jordan, the second day of school!

I get to be in jazz band!	This feels good to be part of a group of people who love music. It sounds a lot better than my elementary school band.	We played the most awesome piece today!
I heard the principal gets in a dunking booth at the end of the school year!	I feel the cool water splash on me as I stand near the booth! It sounds like kids cheering and laughing while trying to dunk the principal!	I felt so much a part of my school today at the end of year bash!
I am so excited to have a locker!	I see the rows and rows of lockers. I can hear the slamming of the doors as people get books and rush off to class.	I keep my locker pretty well clean and organized.
Middle school volleyball!	The gymnasium is painted with a big mascot. I can hear all the squeaking sneakers when we play a game!	It was thrilling to be on the starting line up!
Middle school dances!	I am sure there will be plenty of girls/boys to scope out. Can't wait to dance with Chris!	I was proud how I handed myself today when I was asked to dance!
More independence!	I want to be on the yearbook staff. I can see me going around the school campus taking pictures of people when I am not in class!	I asked Ms. Franks if I could be in yearbook and she said yes!
Award ceremonies!	I hear the clapping and people talking about our academics and sports accomplishments.	I got the Eagle Award!! I have the highest grade point average in science!

The list of middle school positives will pre-pave the road to middle school for you and your child to have wonderful, awesome, successful, and thrilling experiences. Both of you make lists! Do you want your middle school child looking for and attracting positive energy at school? Making the list of positives with feeling statements is one of the most important steps to assisting your child through these years. It is never too late to start positive thinking!

~

Addressing the Negatives

In order to appreciate the positives, we need to address the negatives of middle school. Can they be negative and positive at the same time? I am living proof that positive comes from perceived negative situations! Here is the simple process for addressing negatives:

1. Do not post the list of negatives.

2. Rather, turn each negative statement around into a positive statement.

3. Add feeling statements. Use all five senses as they apply to pre-experience the desired outcome.

4. Transfer ONLY the new positive statements to your on-going positive list.

Negative	Positive	Feeling
I won't know anyone.	It's a great opportunity to meet new people. I will make friends quickly.	I am "freaking out" as I make lots of friends the first day. Acceptance feels great!!!
The teachers might not like me or they will be mean.	I will quickly learn to handle all types of teachers and the expectations.	I feel smart as I understand how each teacher does things. It feels like soaring in the sky when one week, two weeks, three weeks have passed!
I hate social studies.	I will embrace my education and do well in all subjects.	I see an interesting social studies book cover! It smells musty, like it's been stored in a room just waiting for me all summer. The outside feels smooth.
I'm gonna get lost.	I know within two weeks I will be at ease with the school's routine.	I feel very confident at week two because I know my way around the building. It feels like home now.

I might get picked on.	I will have friendly relationships with all students.	It sounds like laughter surrounding me as I joke with everyone. It feels really, really good to know I've been able to accept all my peers for who they are.
I might lose my books.	I will keep my things organized at all times. If I lose my book, I will get others to help me find it.	I feel my hands getting papers out of my binder easily to do my work. It feels like a huge smile inside of me as I know I am in control! It sounds like, "You're doing well!" from my parents.
I will do something stupid and others will laugh at me.	I really accept myself no matter what and realize that everyone will be making mistakes.	It sounds like laughing at myself when I accidentally make a mistake. I hear loving giggling as I discuss what I did with my friends.

In this way, we do not deny the negatives can happen or happened. It is just that now we know to focus on the positive. Ever know someone who is just inherently negative and hangs onto every negative thing possible? It is not much fun to be with them. No matter what you say positively, they will return it with something negative.

A conversation might go like this:

"It's such a nice day to be going to school," stated Student A.

"Yeah, but it's supposed to get really cold by lunch," responded Student B, "and I hate it when I have to go across campus in the cold to biology lab. It just seems that I have to walk across campus on every day that it is freezing."

Then, it's a good thing that you have those warm boots on today," observed Student A.

"Do you see how these boots are ripping right here? I just bought them. Cheap boots. Things just aren't made well anymore."

Student B is in for a very long, hard, and difficult life. Too bad that this student does not know how to control events of life through simple, positive thought energy. I hope someone shows him or her how simple it is to improve one's life.

I cannot express enough about the importance of making this list of middle school concerns. It addresses them before school starts, which alleviates much resistance. Then a pleasant experience can come forth. Continue to add to the lists during the year. Model for your child positive ways to handle all obstacles, challenges, and problems (a.k.a. opportunities) you may experience. Turn them into positive opportunities. What a gift to give your child!

If you already have a middle school student and now realize that you have been negative or you have noticed your child being negative, immediately create these lists. It is never too late to talk about the positives and the positive challenges the middle school experience offers. This process will be especially beneficial as middle school is on the horizon, is currently in your life, is about to end, or is already complete. <u>Here is the really, really good news about this:</u> Positive energy and positive thinking can work in any time and in any direction! Looking back at a middle school experience offers one a review of what happened and an opportunity to change the effect or energy of any situation to a positive one just by thinking about it in a new way.

"HUH?? WHOA. WHAT?? I can change the past?"

No, that is not what I wrote. You can change the *effect* and the *energy* associated with any situation of the past. The past is in the past. It is done. But, many people hold on to the negative feelings about situations, wrong doings, people, and so on, long after these events have passed—even after the people or events are not present anymore! The negative energy stays with them into the present. People do this to themselves unnecessarily. It is really useless, damaging, and makes one feel heavy while focusing on negative energy. It is like toting a full garbage bag 24-7.

The good news is that no matter what has happened in the past, the energy surrounding the situations can be changed and released at any time a person wants to change it. So, if you are a parent of an eighth grader (or whenever needed), review what happened in the middle school years and make a list of situations that feel negative. Beside each one, change the negative statement into a positive statement. What did your child learn? What did your child gain from the experience? For example:

Negative	Positive	Feeling
I got into a fight on the last day of sixth grade.	I stood up for what I felt was right at the time. I learned that I can protect myself.	I feel pride that I didn't back down. I also feel silly about it now, but it was important to me then.
I hate Mr. Pinckney in seventh grade math class because he picked on me a lot.	I learned to ignore irritating teachers and just try to learn as much as I could. I actually started to smile when he was mean.	I feel thrilled that I stayed positive as much as possible during the class while other kids sat around and hated him.
I couldn't go to my eighth grade dance because my aunt died and we had to travel to the funeral.	I learned patience and that family is most important as I experienced family closeness at the funeral.	I am proud of myself for not throwing a hissy fit and staying pretty calm when I was told I couldn't go to my eighth grade dance.
I broke my foot so I couldn't play basketball.	The coach allowed me to remain on the team. I helped with drinks during timeouts and my teammates really appreciated me.	I enjoyed the cooperation feeling when my teammates said thanks for the drinks.
My best friend moved away in the middle of the year.	Jim and I kept in touch for a while. I found a new best friend in Mark.	I feel that I rose up to the challenge of finding a new best friend because Jim had been a really good friend since kindergarten.
I got food thrown on me in the cafeteria.	I learned how to handle embarrassing situations. The "cooler" I was about this, the "cooler" I became.	People came up to me afterward and told me how impressed they were with the way I handled the situation. That felt great!

Sheila was bullying me in the gym locker room during P.E.	I recognized the actions as fear-based. I thought about how I could handle it and got Sheila on my side.	I feel pride I didn't let the bullying get the best of me. I looked behind the actions instead of at them. It's awesome!

Set the example for your child. Just like Gandhi suggested, be the change you wish to see in your child. Here are some suggestions for you to do just that.

- Post your positive lists in more than one visible spot. Refer to them often.

- Post positive messages about life to the ceiling just above your head so that it's the first thing you see when you wake. Consider taping $20, $50, or more (real money or not) in areas you often see like desk drawers, bathroom mirrors, refrigerators, or even the ceiling so that you always focus on and feel rich.

- Hang bright colors in your living and/or work space. Not much money? Discover the remnant bin at the fabric store. Colored streamers work too. Paint is cheap redecorating.

- Surround your living quarters with positive statements about life.

- Post "I AM" statements in many different places like your wallet, your computer, and your bathroom mirror. "I AM ABUNDANT!" "I AM HEALTHY!" "I AM HAVING A REALLY GOOD TIME!" "I AM HAPPY!" "I AM FINANCIALLY SECURE!"

- Surround yourself and your family with positive conversation. Give permission to excuse yourself from gossipy or negative conversations.

- Change your computer passwords to positive words such as abundance, freedom, money, love, peace, light, soaring, achievement, success, blessings, thrilling, and wonderful.

- Have your cell phone display a positive word with your name. You will see it every time you look at your phone.

- E-mail yourself and your child a positive message to be received later.

- Have beautiful images as a screen saver on your computer.

- Hang positive plaques and pictures on the wall. Remove any plaques or pictures that send negative messages, even humorous ones that are inherently negative.

- Clear out clutter. Have a yard sale. Get the tax benefit from a charity donation.

- Clear out sources of negative reading in your home, such as magazines, newspapers, mail, and so forth.

- Clear out negative music. Play music with upbeat melody and lyrics.

- Sing or hum a lively tune as you are in the house.

- Always look for and state the positive of situations.

- Have positive books everywhere in the house, especially in the bathrooms. Does your family like to read while on the "throne"?

- Pay your bills as soon as possible with appreciation. Then focus your thoughts on creating lots of money so that you have plenty of income to *easily* cover everything you desire.

Did that last suggestion feel good to read? Writing positive statements like that one, posting them, and reading them often makes things much better, lighter, cleaner, and fresher! Your good, warm, positive thoughts will lead you to an action (an action you actually will want to do) to bring about that desire! The same is true with your middle school student.

~

An Aid for Focus Power

One such book I have found that is really powerfully positive for all ages is Michael Murphy's personalized books of affirmations.[4] Since we talk to ourselves in all three "persons" (literary term used to describe three points of view), Michael Murphy wrote the book in this manner. Reading one's name in the affirmations does something really powerfully positive. For example:

- I am readily abundant in all areas. (first person)
- You, Lizabeth Jenkins-Dale, are readily abundant in all areas. (second person)
- Lizabeth Jenkins-Dale is readily abundant in all areas. (third person)

Order the personalized book, read it often, and then post positive notes in this same fashion using your name and whatever you would like to see in your life. It is fun to do! All these suggestions create positive energy that can't be denied…even by a middle school student. The human spirit was created by this and for this. To deny the human spirit positive thoughts, which create positive energy, is to deny who and what humans really are.

Think of the opposite just for a very brief moment. What happens when we are thinking and experiencing negativity? Think of something negative. Think of a time when someone criticized you. How do you feel? Uneasy?? The prefix "un" means not, so uneasy means not at ease. The prefix "dis" also means not. Putting dis with ease makes dis-ease. This is disease! Dis ease…disease. Do you understand the importance of your thoughts? Thoughts are incredibly powerful! If a person keeps negative thinking for too long, unease or disease can settle in the body. Now, quick…back to positive thinking—baby giggles: puppy ears; perfect smiles; good grades; loving hugs; warm sun; white, soft sand; rolling hills. You are at peace. Ahhhh…that is better.

When writing and thinking positive thoughts, you will see a change. Middle schoolers sometime cling to negativity because it can get them attention. Habits might be hard to break. Be the role model and do not give up creating a positive environment or talking positively about what is going on at school. Positive energy is too irresistible to resist for long. Remind yourself that we are naturally positive human beings. Negativity is not natural.

If negativity occurs for an extended time and you are concerned, talk to your child's teachers, friends, or doctor, as there may be more to the negativity than just insecurity or middle school jitters. Professional help may be required. It is always better to have things checked out than to remain unsure.

> "So what happens if I do all of those things and my child still has a tough experience in middle school?"

Well, just asking this question indicates a fundamental belief that the negative will rule your child's life. Positive energy is exponentially more powerful than negative energy. If you are worried about all that could go wrong in middle school, then that is where your focus is. Shift your focus, beliefs, and thoughts to, "This is going to be a good year. Things are going to be easy. We are both going to really enjoy this school year. It is going to be fun to meet all the new friends she will make." You get what you focus on. Your thoughts and energies line up exactly with what you will experience. It is quite simple: maintain positive, loving, and fun thoughts and feelings about everything, and that is what you invite into your life.

> "Do you mean we can control other people with our positive thinking? Just by thinking?"

No, you cannot control other people. You *can* control yourself, your thoughts, and your feelings. You can control if you will be present at a negative experience or not. You can control if you are involved in an incident or not. Want traffic jam free driving? Focus on pleasurable driving experiences. Focus on getting to your destination feeling great and on time. Want your child to have a great middle school experience? Focus on feeling good about these years. Focus on her getting along with all of the teachers, getting good grades, and coming home each day with a smile. If your child does the same, he will not be present or be included with conflicts. It is not that these things are not happening. It is just that they will happen when your child is not there!

> "Do you mean that by thinking positive thoughts about whatever we want in life means we will get more of that, and we won't be as likely to be present at the negative events of life?"

Yes! Thinking positively about middle school means that a student just will not be in the vicinity of a conflict if he is focused on having a pleasant middle school experience. She will not be there if someone is upset. He will not be there to witness someone stealing another's stuff. The students who are at these negative events attract them by their thoughts. It is not just by chance. This is very powerful stuff being presented here!

"But what about those kids who are there at a fight, or a disagreement, or those who are at the wrong place at the wrong time?"

Those kids, or any person, attracted such an event by thinking that this could possibly happen to them and holding that negative energy long enough to make it real in his life. Only focusing on what we want in life is the way to ensure it will happen. Out of this focusing will come delightful "pushes" toward pleasant actions that will bring about the positive desired outcomes. Avoid thinking of all the "what ifs." Students can think about positive friendships, awesome grades, ample time to study for tests, easy test reviewing, alert test taking, bountiful free time, solid rest at night, and plentiful money for new clothes.

Here is an example of how to conduct one's life to promote negative situations: A caring, well-intentioned, but misguided parent is concerned with all of life's "what ifs." This person feels it is best to know all the possibilities of life to prepare for, caution children for, and be on the lookout for negative possibilities. There are many avenues, such as TV, Internet, newspapers, talk shows, and other people, from which this parent can find information to feed this focus of thinking, worrying, reading, hearing, and discussing about all the things that could possibly go wrong and have gone wrong. This is the type of parent who will see or experience negatives because it is the focus and attracting vibration. Then, those exact unwanted negatives are watched on TV, read about, and discussed with others, continuing the cycle! A parent such as this one spends daily energy in a constant state of worry. A parent such as this one spends daily energy seeking negative news to bring to the family to warn them. A parent such as this one spends daily energy attracting those unwanted things. There is such a focus on all the "what ifs" of life, that those "what ifs" will appear, thus reinforcing the need to remain in that state of worry, caution, and protective stance. No wonder this parent gets tired by the end of the day!

"Ugh! I can feel the heaviness of that last paragraph. It doesn't feel good to me. But, I know that I have been like that parent, worrying about my children, worrying about what might happen to them, worrying about their futures. It all feels very heavy right now. Yuck. I don't want to live my life like that."

Unfortunately, evidence of such a focus will show up in life and will reinforce what the parent says to be true. Often, negative experiences, near misses, turbulent encounters, and difficult situations appear. This parent is projecting "life is scary" and the world is responding likewise.

How different life would be with a complete focus on just what is wanted! The parent would be safe in a completely different city than the one where a shooting occurs. The parent would be happily driving on a completely different street or driving at a completely different time than one with problems such as an accident. Helpful people would always be present for this parent while touring a foreign country. Eating at restaurants would always be pleasant experiences. The parent would be at a football game where every player did their best with no injuries. The parent would have a productive day at work with all going smoothly. Even the temperamental vending machine would surrender the selected product easily. The parent would have positive relationships with everyone and everything. Anyone who maintains a positive focus attracts the best life has to offer!

Here is an example of how to conduct one's life to promote positive situations: A caring and well-intentioned parent is concerned with all of life's positive possibilities. This person feels it is best to think about and feel the joy of life, the "zip" in life, and the freedom of life. The desire is to anxiously await the conversations with her children about all the good things that happened during the day, discuss the visualizations of the greatness that could be for them and for the family, and explain the exciting things that are up and coming. A parent such as this avoids those avenues of negative input. This person is quite picky about which topics and which friends to converse with. This parent spends daily energy in a state of "all is well" and "life is great" or "things are only going to get better." This parent spends daily energy maintaining a lookout for people being kind to one another, observing how well things work, such as the synchronicity of the traffic lights, and appreciating the beautiful cloud formations that are ever present and ever changing.

If I experience anything other than what I want, I know that somewhere I am projecting that focus and I take the time to adjust my focus as soon as possible. Depending on the subject, it may take me a few minutes to change my focus. It may take me days to change my focus. It may take me longer to change my focus, but I know that I have the control over the events of my life with my thoughts and feelings. Now, that is power!

We Are Magnetic

Everyone is a powerful magnet. What do we, as individuals, want to attract from the world's choices? We bring it to us by focus. Are magnets picky about the metal object they stick to? No. Whatever is present and magnetic they stick to it. As a human magnet, we do have a choice what we attract. Be sure your "magnetic" thoughts are positive because whatever your thoughts are, they will stick to you!

> "What if many people want the same thing and they each attract it by the same magnetic thought choice. What if, then, one more person desires it, but there's no more?"

Good question! Think about it for a minute…there are billions of people in this world. Everyone has desires. Someone wants a fancy sports car, while another wants a new sturdy bike. Someone wants to travel, while another wants to stay home and sell artwork. Someone wants a mountain house, while another wants an apartment. There is plenty of money, stuff, experiences, space, and resources for all the desires of each person in the world. Shortage is an illusion. There is plenty of everything for everyone's desires.[5]

> "Oh my! Now, that is a new twist on this subject! Shortage is an illusion? There is plenty for all? That hasn't been my experience or the world's experience. I can easily find shortages with even the most basic life necessities. How can a hungry belly be an illusion? Try explaining that one!"

I will briefly explain this very interesting subject here, but I encourage you to read other, more thorough sources of information about unlimited abundance for everyone. Remember, your focus is your experience. Hungry bellies are caused by a focus on lack. There are times when a large group of humans are focusing on one thing and it becomes a huge problem. Then the media broadcasts it into many, many homes, often dramatizing it with music and close up shots as people get emotional. This broadcasting of the problem makes the problem bigger because more and more people are now focused on the problem. What would happen in our homes, in our communities, in our countries, in the world, if everyone watched TV shows focused on abundance, plenty, happiness, peace, and prosperity? What would we find in the world then?

We humans are creators. If we desire something, we can create a way to have it. Gandhi did it. Thomas Edison did it. Martin Luther King, Jr. did it. Alexander Graham Bell did it. Babe Ruth did it. Jackie Robinson did it. Henry Ford did it. Oprah Winfrey's doing it. I am doing it. You are doing it. In fact, everyone is doing it... whether they know it or not!

There is no shortage because we can focus on the desire so much that a way will be discovered. And, there are many unknowns yet to be discovered! An example of this is in the late 1600s when Antonie van Leeuwenhoek, a pioneer in microbiology, first saw microorganisms with his self-created microscopes. This opened a huge, previously invisible world to us! This led to the practice of washing hands between patients. This led to wonderful creations like antibiotics.

Out of our frustration with oil dependency, as well as the effects of pollution, we desired new ways to move from one place to another. Eco-friendly vehicles are becoming mainstream now. Humans communicate using electronic devices unknown a mere ten years ago. In 1975, Bill Gates, co-founder of Microsoft, desired, "a computer on every desk and in every home." People laughed at him because computers were large, bulky pieces of machinery, taking up multiple rooms in offices. Computers small enough to fit on a desk? Ha! Mine fits on my lap. Some fit in a hand!

The world conducts money transactions in many different ways than just a hundred years ago. We will always create new ways to obtain what we want if we focus on our desires. Also, there is plenty just for you and you alone. Your desire is your desire and it exists because you thought about it. And now because you "birthed" your desire, it is out there waiting just for you. No one else is going to get it. And, when you obtain your desire, you are not taking anything away from anyone else's desire. Yours is yours. Theirs is theirs.[6] Again, I say, there is plenty for everyone! Shortage is an illusion.

> "Hmmm…I'll have to file that one in a mental folder to ponder later. Plenty for all is such a contradiction to what I've been taught and have observed. I do like it, though. It feels so much better than shortage. It feels empowering. It feels good to know that my desire is mine and is waiting on me to get it. It is refreshing to know that no one will take it from me. It feels like a more relaxing and peaceful way to live life."

YUP! Powerful stuff, right? Some people will understand and embrace all of this because they will see the benefit—we create the lives we experience. This is creation! It is wonderful to be in creative control, right? But, others may feel cautious about it because all the responsibility for one's life is on the *one* self. There is no room for blaming someone else or something else. Not only is there no room to blame another person or another thing, but also there is no room to blame anyone who *wants* to get into conflicts. Focusing on others who purposely entertain conflicts would bring that thought energy into your focus. You can easily think about those who like conflict, but you can also just as easily think about peace, freedom, liberty, and safety. So, appreciate knowing (for brief moments) about conflicts so that you can now focus on peace.

> "Huh? Appreciate knowing about conflicts so that I can focus on peace? Please explain."

How can you choose to focus on peace unless you know about conflict? It is knowing that the two exist (peace and conflict) that gives you the opportunity to know that you can choose which one you want. Condemning the one you do not like is bringing it into your focus. Uh oh…not good, right? Simply acknowledge that conflict exists for the purpose of understanding peace. Then, focus on peace without giving the other any blame, judgment, or further attention.

> "OK. This one is a tricky one. Not give the woes of our world any blame, judgment, or attention? That is pretty hard. There's so much wrong with our world."

Well, there certainly is much to worry, blame, fear, judge, and concern yourself with if you are looking for these things. By accepting these things as part of the world and making a choice to shift focus, you know you can choose happy, peaceful, joyful, friendly, and amazing things instead. The world is filled with dualities—up-down, happy-sad, hot-cold, wet-dry, right-left, female-male, me-others, on-off, separate-together, rich-poor, here-there, visible-invisible, peace-conflict, and many, many more. Appreciating each one as an opportunity to decide your focus is the purpose for the duality, and is powerful!

~

You Already Are Powerfully Focusing

All of this is not as difficult as it may seem. You already focus your thoughts on what you want in certain areas of your life. Are you picky about the car you drive, the movies you see, the friends you keep, the foods you eat, and the clothes you wear? The same is true about the customs you enjoy, the shoes you wear, the education path you take, and the plants you purchase. Surely there are plenty of shoes that do not suit your tastes when shoe shopping. Do we blame, judge, or pay attention to them? Do we call the news media to make a big deal about the undesirable shoes? Do we demand the shoes be removed from the shelves? No, we simply go on with the pursuit of shoes that are pleasing to us. It is part of the fun to find that one special pair of shoes from the vast selection!

When deciding what to order at a restaurant from the menu, do you ask for a menu only with the items that are to our liking? Or, do you find it interesting that there are items on the menu that you do not like? You are able to make decisions from the offerings on the menu despite the variety. You focus on what you desire and order those things to have a pleasing meal.

Would a college student who is studying biology demand that all English courses, art courses, and accounting courses be removed from the school's catalog of educational offerings? No, the student focuses on his or her personal choice of biology courses. It may happen, however, that this person might want to change from biology to accounting. The student would then be grateful that so many choices are available, that the courses were not eliminated, and that the choices were there in the first place to give rise to a desire to change from biology to accounting!

Ponder football. The game requires that all players work together, but focus on different tasks for the betterment of the whole team. The receiver's focus is to run the right pattern, catch the ball, and run up the field while avoiding being tackled by opposing players. The offensive lineman's job is to block an oncoming player's attempt to tackle the quarterback before the ball is thrown to the receiver. The quarterback, as the offensive linemen are blocking oncoming opponents nearby, must scan the field for the positions of the receivers, decide which one has the best opportunity to catch the ball, and throw the ball to a spot where the running receiver will be shortly. Talk about focus! What would happen if the quarterback focused on what he does not want (to be "sacked") and not on what he does want (to complete a pass)? What if the oncoming opponents were removed because it was demanded by the quarterback? Would the game have as much interest if the quarterback had plenty of time without pressure to throw the ball to a receiver? No. The excitement is present because the quarterback throws amazing passes in the midst of pressure. If the quarterback can focus on what he wants in the midst of opponents coming at him, can we do the same?

Do you like amusement parks? Do you love the "rush" of the scary, loud, fast, thrilling rides? Do you crave that free fall feeling? Do you wait in the long lines just to experience going backward from great heights even if it is only for a short period of time? Well...good for you. I do not. I cannot physically tolerate any of those experiences. My stomach turns when I even think about it. I get woozy just standing on the ground watching these spectacular sights. When I go to amusement parks, which I do every summer, I am quite focused on what rides I will consider. I am diligent in resisting anyone's urging, pleading, or begging for me to join them on *those* rides. Do I demand to go to amusement parks with only the rides I enjoy? Do I demand that the rides I don't like be removed? No. I enjoy watching others before and after the scary ride. It makes me glad I am not on the ride! I love to watch their expressions of nervousness before the ride takes off and their smiles, excitement, clapping, whooping and hollering when they return.

Got a tattoo? Want a tattoo? It doesn't matter your opinion on the subject, because either opinion provides an opportunity to explain this subject further. If person A does not want a tattoo, person A does not get one! If Person A is not fascinated by those with tattoos or want to know more about tattoos, then tattoos do not enter Person A's life. A happy Person A is not running around bad-mouthing those who have tattoos, but observes that some people choose to have ink injected under their skin by artists and some people do not. Person A has already made the personal decision to not get a tattoo *and* appreciates the variety of life at the same time.

When I finally completed the divorce process, I was so tremendously relieved that I seriously contemplated several ways to celebrate. I thought about getting a very small tattoo. I pondered getting a belly button piercing. And, I made plans to go parachuting with a colleague. Yup! Together with my newfound knowledge and the release from the divorce process, I was almost floating on air! I wanted to do something out of the ordinary - for me, that is. I am extremely thankful to this day that such choices existed for me to contemplate, as I could feel the exhilaration of each possibility. In the end, even though I did not go through with any of the choices, I can still reminisce how I felt at that time of my life. I appreciate all the choices of life and am glad variety exists.

The Wonderful Kitchen Metaphor

Another way to present this concept is to take from the Esther and Jerry Hicks-Abraham metaphor for life as a kitchen that has every ingredient available to make infinite creations.[7] Isn't this awesome? Everything is provided for us in this kitchen (our world) to make anything we would like…to make infinite creations! Wow! It is all in this kitchen, which is all of the diversity of life!

By birth, you are in the kitchen having a good time creating. You look at all the ingredients and select the ones you want. You delight in the spectacular variety of ingredients! You put your selected ingredients into your creation, taste your creation, and declare it wonderfully yummy. This is just like life. What do you want to include in your life to make it delicious? You carefully select what you want in your life from the vast choices and declare it wonderful!

Thinking negatively is similar to being in this kitchen, and while you are making your creation, you notice some of the ingredients that you do not want in your creation. You become worried that because the ingredients are simply in the kitchen that they might end up in what you are doing. You complain about them being in the kitchen.

You would rather they not be in the kitchen. You wage anti-ingredient protests for these ingredients. You try to throw them in the trash only to find that there are now more in your cupboards than ever before! You talk to others about these horrible, in your opinion, ingredients. You worry and you worry and you focus on these ingredients that you do not want. When your creation is finished, you realize that you inadvertently put those unwanted ingredients into there because you were so focused on them! What you have made does not taste very good now, and you are unhappy about it. You declare it is the ingredients' fault your creation is not wonderful. Now, you are determined to have those ingredients removed! On and on it goes…

Where is the focus of the person in the kitchen of life who is supposed to be creating joyously from the wonderful, vast selection of ingredients?

Had the cook maintained focus only on the ingredients wanted, everything would be exactly the way she wanted it to be. Since there are so many other cooks in the kitchen of life, the kitchen has every ingredient possible. Someone else might want to use those ingredients even if one cook does not think they taste very good. It may happen that the cook will change his mind and want to use those ingredients in the future. Yes, the cook may change his opinion of those ingredients some day! Then, he will bring those ingredients into his focus, thoughts, and energy.

I hope the metaphor used so often by Esther and Jerry Hicks-Abraham helps you to understand about the power of positive, focused thinking. I also hope you can see how life supports you, is *for* you, and is to be fun, joyful, and happy.

There are all kinds of metaphors that can be used to illustrate the truth that we are in control of the events, people, and happenings in our lives. Be the pilot of your airplane, flying through the stages of your life to your desired destinations. As the pilot, you not only get to decide the destinations (your fun, goals, achievements, relationships, and desires you want to experience), but you also get to choose the passengers (those you choose to be your friends and acquaintances as you travel through your life) and flight crew (those who are going to help you get where you want to go). You know that there is no need to complain about not arriving yet at the destination because you know you will get there—you are the pilot! You know not to drop bombs on all the undesirable (in your opinion) destinations you will fly over as you travel. Those are for other pilots, and maybe in the future, you will change your mind and want to fly to those destinations. In addition, you understand that at any time, you can change your destination if it is not exactly the experience you wanted. Dropping off and inviting new passengers are also your choices because this is your plane, your flight plan, your destination.

Think of it as being the video game player of your life. Your child will love this one! You have the controller. There is no way for anyone to ever get the controls from you unless you give them the controls. You decide the games (opportunities, experiences) you want to play. You decide what happens in your game. You decide the elements of the game such as type of car, other characters, your personal characteristics, your strengths, paths, and so on. When an "adversary" comes your way, what do you do? You go another way. You avoid it. You choose another path. You focus on the end result and ignore the adversary. You understand that the adversary makes the game fun. You don't demand video games without some sort of challenge, do you? It would become boring quickly if there was no "adversary"! In real life, this analogy gets even better because you actually can control the events of your life by focusing on the fact that everything is going to go your way. Even though video games have preprogrammed adversaries, life is not preprogrammed. You are in control.

Want more? Be the sports player on your field (your life). You get to choose the playing objects, the players, the coach, and so on. You understand the perfection of your choices and you know not to complain about the other sports played by other players, as you might want to try them some day. You simply focus on the sport you are playing right now. There is no need to complain about the competition, as that is the very thing making your sport exciting! That is the very thing spurring you on to be better and better! As a sports player, you are thankful for competition.

Be the truck driver of your highway (your life). You choose your truck, your travel direction, your truck stops, your passengers, the cargo you haul, your arrival time, your speed, and so on. As a happy trucker on your highway, you know to enjoy the scenery as you progress to your destination rather than complain or become frustrated because you are not there yet. You also know to focus on your path only and ignore other highways leading to other destinations.

Be the artist of your creation (your life). You choose your artist supplies, your style, your completion speed, your medium (plaster, clay, paper, or canvas), and your end result. As a content artist, you choose to focus only on your artistic choices and know they are good instead of writing an editorial in the newspaper demanding the elimination of all the other artistic options you do not prefer. The artist in you understands that artistic creation (life) is a process, and through the refining of the materials (experiences), you create new desires of creation and all of it is good.

Be the author of your story (life). You write the stories, and if you do not like the way it is ending, you can rewrite a new ending. You can write a whole new story! You can change characters and events and settings any time you want with the thoughts (your focus) that come forth from you. As an author, you don't get upset because the book isn't done yet. You LOVE the process of writing the book! You get an absolute thrill from how the ideas, characters, events, and interactions among all the story elements come together almost magically to create a most tantalizing, intriguing, and "I can't put the book down" story! Once you complete a book, you relish in the satisfaction of those who love it, learn from it, and extract joy from it too. Then, onto the next story you want to create!

Here is one more metaphor to explain how to have the life you really want, and how to model, show, and assist your child to have the middle school experience he wants! Think of life as a stage and the director of the play (life) is your child.[8] He gets to make all the decisions. He gets to create his life. Who does he ask to be on his stage? What experiences does your child invite to be in his play? Any middle schooler would love and easily understand this metaphor. The idea of being director of one's life is very attractive!

If the director invites someone or some experience to be on his stage, it might not always be a leading role in his play or in a main scene. It might even be a conflict, a problem, a difficulty. As the director of his play, he always has choices. He can view the person and event as a learning experience, and now with more wisdom, he can release the person and event from his play by focusing on something new that feels better. The director has that control!

With complete knowing what the you (the director) focus on becomes, what you feel is, and what you think exists on your stage, what are you going to say, focus, feel, or think to make your play the most wonderful for you? Are you going to be pretty picky about what you say, focus, feel, and think about? I would! Your middle schooler will too.

> "Thank you for all the metaphors. I think I am starting to understand this. What I experience is because of my focus. If my focus is just on what I want, then I can make it happen pretty quickly. If my focus is on both what I want and what I don't want, then I get some of both. If my focus is on what I want because I fear something happening to me, then I am really focused on what I don't really want. So, if I focus on what I want just because it's fun to want it, then I can have the life I desire."

Yes. It is that simple. Add great emotion behind your thoughts and it becomes much easier. In other words, be really excited about receiving your desires. Visualize what it will be like and be happy about it! Adding the emotion with your focus adds power to your wishes. You will be amazed how your middle schooler will embrace this way of creating desires. You will be amazed how your middle schooler can create a wonderful life.

SIX

The Icing on the Middle School Cake

Ask any kid about cake and they will tell you that the best part is the icing. I have to admit, I agree. There is still a part of me that watches as the cake is cut and I long for the piece with lots of icing. The rich, sweet, creamy taste is too irresistible! Icing merged with the cake texture makes for sensory delight. Well, after all this explaining about your thoughts and feelings, the effect they have on your life, and how you can have total control of your life, here is the icing on this subject…the best part!

Be thankful. Yes, that's it. The icing on the middle school cake is to be thankful for everything. Simple, huh? Be thankful for the variety of students, for your child gets to choose his friends. Be thankful for the existing clubs and for those yet to be created, for your child gets to determine which ones suit her. Be thankful for the teachers, for your child learns who he is as he "bounces" off each teacher's personality.

See? It is pretty easy, isn't it? Does it not feel good? With all this positive thinking and thankfulness, you naturally "open" yourself to receiving the good stuff you want in your life. Gratitude brings more of what you want quicker than anything else! THAT is why it is the icing on the cake! Gratitude is what makes visualization, or focusing on what you want out of life, super effective!

Take Gratitude to an Intimate and Intense Level

This gratitude thing can be taken to an even higher level of thankfulness. Can you feel the awesome positive energy as I delve into the following? Be thankful for the school building in which your child learns to navigate through the halls to get to classes on time, for there were many, many conversations, meetings, and plans even before one ounce of dirt was moved. Be thankful because school board members, zoning board workers, architects, community members, builders, and machinery workers were involved with building the school. Be thankful because once the building process started there were many hands making sturdy halls. Who made the cement blocks? Who delivered the thousands of cement blocks? Can you appreciate the talents of those placing, aligning, and securing cement block after cement block? Be thankful for the ones who painted the halls, hung the lights, ran the electrical cords, installed the pencil sharpeners, fitted the blinds, delivered the desks, hung the doors, installed the toilets, positioned the flooring, lifted the sinks into place, mounted the mirrors, installed the fans, placed the windows, set up the public address system, and secured the light fixture covers. Be thankful for the taxpayers' money, which paid for the blocks, paint, lighting, mirrors, fans, windows, sinks, and so on, and compensated all the building artisans. Whew! After all that, it is really hard to feel negative because so many people and so much effort came together to create space for children to learn. *That* is something to be thankful for!

Here is more! Be thankful for the shoes on your child's feet as she walks down the school halls. Be thankful for the many persons involved with creating those shoes on her feet: designers, seamstresses, sewing machine company employees, rubber plant growers and harvesters, cotton growers and harvesters, glue company employees, shoelace company employees…on and on it goes! The point is to go deep into appreciation, thankfulness, and gratitude.

What happens is nothing short of wonderful. You become aware of so much more than your tiny world. You realize how intricately our world is entwined with all the parts of it. From this place of wonderment, you can create the life you desire quickly. You will feel lighter. From this place of "en-light-ment," you can create the life you desire quickly. You will feel peaceful. From this place of peace, you can create the life you desire quickly. You will feel all is well. From this place of wellness, you can create the life you desire quickly. You will feel no resistance to creating the life you want. From this place of freedom, you can create the life you desire quickly.

> "So…I think I see a relationship between the way I feel and my ability to create the life I want. Is this true? If I am in a good mood, I can be a better creator? When I am happy, I make the path straighter for me to access the things I want in my life? It seems that gratitude is such a strong feeling that it's the best one with which to bring forth the desires of my heart?"

Gratitude does encompass all the positive emotions. It includes happy, peace, understanding, compassion, and joy because it includes all the events of your life.

> "Uh…all events of my life? Gratitude? Joy? For all the events of my life? I don't know if I can feel gratitude for *all* the events of my life. Please help me understand this."

I have gratitude for all the events of my life because I can look back at them and appreciate their influences in my life and the way they have brought me to this point in time. I like where I am, so I am grateful for all the events that preceded this moment. Gratitude is always a feeling to place oneself in alignment for personal power.

> "I can see how gratitude is available to some people. What about people who are raped or abused or have experienced the murder of someone close to them? I'll have to take some time to ponder the events of my life to see how and if I can appreciate the effects and, therefore, the gratitude I can hold for each event. But, what about those who have had really, really horrible things happen to them?"

Since I am not them, I cannot answer for them. I truly cannot totally understand the depth of those experiences. How I can answer your question is that each event in life is a chance to realize something new. These people have opportunities to realize how those events happened to them and how to avoid them from this point forward. These people have opportunities to use the experiences as powerful vehicles to help themselves, help others, and to realize their own personal powers. What did Loretta Scott King do when her husband was assassinated? What did Tina Turner do after being abused by her husband for years? Do you know anyone who was raped, survived, and triumphed as a result? Oprah Winfrey is an excellent example of choosing something different for her life, overcoming the negative effects of multiple rape experiences, and using the experiences to help others. Oprah Winfrey believes in the tremendous power of gratitude and she has many articles about this subject on her Web site.

Kim Jenkins wrote an article in 2009 entitled, "Manifesting Desires with a10/10 Journal."[9] Her article gives powerful reasons for keeping a gratitude journal, or what she calls her "What Went Right Today" journal. Ms. Jenkins accredits Matthew Ferry for the "10/10" gratitude journal idea. It's writing ten good things about your day and writing ten things you want to attract into your life. This simple design is very powerful for anyone, including middle school students!

So, getting back to the original question of how to respond to the really horrible events of life.... There are many ways of addressing those negative situations in life. I choose to look for the positive effects my events had on me, forgive those (including me) who apparently hurt me, accept total responsibility for my part in creating the situations, focus on a new way of living, and take my power back when I realize that I am in control of all the events of my life. When I acknowledged my responsibility in creating the situations, I became powerful. I became creator! When I released all blame on the others, I released me from having to hold it there on them. Whew! One less thing to do! When I released all blame on me, I released myself and became free to love myself. When I shifted my focus to what I wanted in my life, I did two HUGE things: (1) I did not have to think about, look at, or deal with the apparent negative events any more—no more rehashing the sequence of events, no more being victim and telling others about it; and, (2) I attracted new positive things, people, and events into my life. So, yes, I am grateful!

I bet I am more grateful for my husband and our marriage than many wives because of my previous experiences. So, yes, I am grateful for those experiences! Would a parent of a murdered child deem life more valuable than the rest of us? Could a woman who can't or has great difficulty conceiving hold precious her children more than those who easily conceived or accidentally conceived children? Does an amputee enjoy the ability to run more than the rest of us? Does a blind person marvel at the sense of touch, taste, smell, and sound more than the rest of us? Would a sick person desire health more than the rest of us? Could a low income person who attracts money appreciate wealth more than those who have it bequeathed to them? Does an abused person relish safety more than the rest of us? Can one who has experienced incest delight in positive family interactions more than the rest of us? Might one who has experienced murder of another savor each and every day more than the rest of us? Can we transform negative events into useful, powerful, and life transforming events? Yes! Can negative events even become sources for gratitude? Yes! We all have choices for our responses to the events of our lives. That is good news, and I am grateful for it!

SEVEN

It's Not Just About the Teachers

Ponder your own middle school experience. What do you remember most? When asked, most almost immediately start telling teacher stories—"mean" teachers, "easy" teachers, "fun-to-trick" teachers, "strict" teachers, "funny" teachers, "weird" teachers, "eccentric" teachers, "pretty" teachers, and "old" teachers. Well, I am sure you have your own middle school teacher stories. But, it is not just about the teachers, however. There is much more...much, much more!

For example, early in my teaching career, I learned an important rule about *any* school: The two most important people are the receptionist and the day porter. Is this surprising to you? Did you expect me to write that the principal and the vice principal are the two most important people in any school? Perhaps, your child's homeroom teacher and the librarian? By acknowledging the receptionist and day porter's utmost importance, and them sensing my sincere respect, a symbiotic relationship always resulted. When I was in the front office, I tried to assist the receptionist by answering telephones and addressing parent concerns as I was able. I kept my needs to a minimum for the day porter, who was always quite busy maintaining a large building. When he asked for help, I willingly sent him my best class volunteers—much to their delight! In return, I received special treatment in the form of extra copy numbers on the copier prior to the new quarter, permission to use school supplies freely, fast track teacher materials ordering, forgiveness when receipted monies were not completed on time, pertinent information ahead of time, scheduling perks (e.g., my team grazed on the PTA food first or preferential scheduling on picture day), student vomit removed promptly, and needed supplies delivered to my room in a timely manner. Yes, early on, I realized that these two people ran the school. They were the ones really in charge!

> "Hmmmm…this is a new twist on the subject of middle school because when I think about schools, I always think about teachers and principals, but really not anyone else. Interesting. There *are* many more people in the building beside teachers! Day porters, receptionists, teacher assistants…um…having a hard time here listing them…who else?"

I will highlight the numerous people involved with a school including those already mentioned. It is pertinent, as well, to acknowledge the *things* involved with a school in addition to the people.

Remember, all these influences are optional for every student. Students can focus on what they want to reduce or eliminate any potentially negative influence. Students can look for the positive with each of these influences or complain how awful each one is. As a parent be cognizant of these influencing factors in a middle school because any school's environment is vast. If your child comes home from school irritable and complains about a teacher or two, there might be more to the irritation than just the teachers.

These influencing variables include, but are not limited to:

Peers

- Other students – These are the #1 influencers on your child's day. With adjustment to one's focus, other students can become the #1 positive influencers on your child.

- Recent team sports game results – The game the night before can have residual effect, still lingering the next day. It may manifest in an inflated ego sitting in the chair next to your child, extra energy in the building, or an irritable player receiving negative feedback due to a missed winning shot.

- Pre-game discussions – Middle school energy levels rocket sky high prior to games and events. Were comments pleasing or irritating to your child?

- Boys and girls – Yes, I know this is obvious, but it needs to be mentioned here in this chapter. We are discussing middle school students, right? Boys, girls, boyfriends, girlfriends, break-ups, "going with" or "going out," flirting, "stealing" another's interest…need I write more??

Administration

- Principal – Usually, principals address the student body each morning. With what kind of energy is the day started? Is this person friendly? Accessible? Visible to students?

- Principal's relationship with staff – What is the tone? Are staff members relaxed around the principal? Relaxed school administrators create relaxed teachers, which create relaxed students.

- Vice principal(s) – Usually, Vice Principals handle school discipline. Are they positively reinforcing wanted behaviors or burned out handling issues? Do they attempt to establish rapport with all students, even the well-behaved students?

Educators

- Regular education teachers – These people are all over the school, and all of them are influencing factors, even if not your child's current teachers. All teachers are responsible for all students and may interact with your child for a variety of reasons.

- Special area teachers – Are these teachers excited about their subjects (commonly: chorus, strings, band, yearbook, art, physical education, computers)? Do they project "regular education teacher" images so that all students respect them as "real" teachers?

- Media center specialist, a.k.a. the librarian – Media center specialists are usually grouped with the special area teachers, but I wanted to bring particular attention to this person in a middle school building. The media center specialist plays such an important role for student academic support. Is this person friendly? Does the library have a peaceful atmosphere? Are there many places to read? Is it easy to obtain information? How is crowd control handled? Is the library accessible to all students and when? Is this person very willing to help students?

- Guidance counselor(s) – Are these people visibly present and accessible? Do they emanate "I'm on your side" vibes to students?

- Special education teachers – These teachers have extra understanding for children, which always amazed me. Usually, these teachers extend their understanding to regular education students.

- Intermittent teachers – Some students receive weekly services such as speech lessons. The district hires fulltime teachers who travel among many schools to help a few students at each school.

- Teacher assistants – These people are all over the school and are influencing factors as they enter classrooms to assist children with special needs, and they may lend a hand to a regular education child, which might cause some embarrassment if the help is unwanted.

- Substitutes – All these people vary greatly—some are nice, some are mean, some just want a paycheck, some actually want to teach, some are old, some are very young, but all of them are subject to student misbehavior in middle schools. This can cause stress with those students who want to learn every day and/or who are concerned about whole class consequences at the hands of a few.

- Student teachers – These people may vary from young college students to older college students. These people may vary from once a week teaching experiences up to sixteen-week continuous teaching experiences. No matter the situation, they are people in the building learning the teacher role, which means their inexperience may be quite evident. Student teachers are usually nervous, which may lead them to make decisions different than that of a more experienced teacher. This is part of the learning process for them.

- Teacher-student ratio – This is dictated mostly by economics. It is partly controlled by the principal because some popular classes (e.g., honors classes) may have high teacher-student ratio while some "review" classes may have small teacher-student ratio. Does the teacher-student ratio make your child feel comfortable? Does it feel overcrowded and cramped? Does it feel too small?

Support Staff

- Receptionist(s) – Are these people friendly to students? Do these people automatically respect students or automatically assume all students are impolite? What is the tone of the school's front office toward children?

- Attendance clerk – How does this person interact with students occasionally arriving tardy? How is the admission slip/late slip given to students?

- Bookkeeper(s) – This person is usually a behind the scenes person, but still an influencing person, as monies are collected in schools for various events, such as dances, field trips, fund raisers, and spirit t-shirts.

- School nurse – Is this person male or female? How does your child feel about the sex of the school nurse? Female students may not feel comfortable with asking for feminine products from a middle school male nurse. How are students greeted when they enter the nurse's office? Are ailments, physical complaints, and medicine disbursement handled professionally? Is the nurse's office clean, accessible, and well stocked? In other words, does your child feel cared for appropriately?

- Experience level – The experience level of any person in the building influences the manner in which situations and interactions are conducted. A person beginning a career may be more uptight and nervous than an experienced person. A person beginning a career may make judgment calls that will differ from how that same person may react ten years down the chronological road.

- Experience in the building – How long has any one person worked in your child's school? Continuity usually offers "comfortableness," so these people have an ease about them. Is there high turnover each year of staff and teachers? There is much to be said about a school with faculty and staff who renew their contracts year after year.

> "Your point about experience in the building is right on. It's always so obvious who is comfortable and who is not."

So as a parent, how can you empower new-to-the-building people or even new-to-the-teaching-career people? It is in your best interest, and your child's, to help foster a pleasant experience for everyone in the building. All employees are important. Everyone wants to feel safe and included. Parents can really positively boost their child's school environment by assisting everyone in the school setting by providing welcome baskets, placing a cookie or flower on all employee desks the first day of school, or assigning a buddy parent to a new teacher to perform periodic check ins. I will elaborate on other strategies at the end of the section, but, first, here are more influences.

Cafeteria

- Cafeteria workers – With what kind of energy is the food prepared and presented to students? Lunch is a huge deal to middle school students. Hopefully, your child's school cafeteria workers enjoy and have a healthy understanding of middle schools students.

- Cleanliness of cafeteria – Gooey or clean tables? Are tables cleaned between classes? Are students allowed to socialize during this time? How is dismissal handled—orderly or chaotically?

- Arrangement of cafeteria tables – Believe it or not, this is a biggie. Availability of seating, ease of obtaining food, and allowing of socialization are all really important.

- The quality of lunch and snack food – Kids know when they are given cheap or good quality food. This influencing factor helps to create the atmosphere both in the classroom and in the cafeteria starting waaaaaaayyyy back in the classrooms where stomachs begin to growl.

- Lunch time – *When* lunch is can be just as important as *what* lunch is! Does your child become grumpy when hungry? Is your child sluggish with a belly full of food? Both can cause issues at school.

Building Support Staff

- Day porter(s) – These people clean, repair, install, and distribute school items during the day. Are they happy or grumpy? Do they use students' help when needed? Students love to help the day porters!

- Nighttime janitorial staff – These people often appear before school is over to begin the thorough school cleaning. Are they friendly? Do they complain about the condition of the school at the end of the day before kids leave?

- Intermittent school building workers – The district hires full time electricians, plumbers, builders, and welders who circulate among schools to address building issues that are too large for the day porter to handle. Are they friendly? Do they ignore or look "through" kids as they complete a job?

Building

- Environmental health of the building – Does the school building smell good? Are common issues absent, such as rust, insects, and mold?

- Number and proximity of bathrooms and water fountains to students – These are important places to middle school students. How often are bathroom breaks and when? How are "I really gotta go!" emergencies handled? Is there a water fountain located near a bathroom and how many? Are the bathrooms kept clean, free of graffiti, pleasant smelling, and well lighted? Do students have to travel far to find bathrooms from classrooms? Do teachers often complain how long students are away from instruction due to bathroom breaks?

- The layout of the building – Is the building complicated or easy to navigate? Are students rushing to get to classes on time?

- Temporary classrooms – These are referred as trailers and are utilized due to overcrowded school buildings or construction of new school buildings. Some trailers are nice; some are definitely not! If your child has classes in trailers, what are the conditions of the trailers? How far must your child walk to the trailers? Does the teacher allow extra time to arrive punctually? What provisions are made to accommodate students walking in wet, hot, or cold weather? It is really hard to concentrate on school lessons with cold, wet feet. Are the trailers located in a secured area? How many classes are in trailers? Does your child feel isolated from friends?

- Lockers – Do lockers open with ease? When can students utilize lockers during the day? Are lockers assigned logically, meaning do tall kids get top lockers while shorter kids get bottom lockers? How are lockers secured?

- Hallway width – This is a huge issue if the halls are narrow. Kids bump into each other more often with limited space, which can cause tension. Middle school kids like traveling arm to arm so wide halls are especially pleasant to them.

- Hallway movement patterns – This is very important to maintaining peace in hallways with large numbers of students moving to classes at once. Do teachers actively monitor hallway movement? Are there definite patterns? How do kids know in what manner to move to the next class?

- School building - Sometimes the building does strange things like sense a fire that's not there, flicker the lights for no apparent reason, ring hallway bells at the wrong time, burst a water pipe, back up the toilets, leak rain water, trap students in the elevator, and many more "mysterious" acts. These seemingly small occurrences cause students to feel and act "off."

- Wall colors – Simply, irritating or pleasing? Are wall paint and decorations in good condition?

- Classroom seating – Are the chairs, desks, and tables pleasing or uncomfortable to your child? Where is your child seated in the room? Under a vent? By a window? By the classroom door? Near the heater or air conditioner? Near or far away from the front of the room?

- Windows – Are there just enough to be pleasing or too many to be hot, too bright, and too distracting? What is the condition of the windows? Are there blinds and are the blinds in good condition?

- Fire regulations – Does every room have an emergency escape route map posted? Is this practiced monthly at different times of the day? Any day there is a fire drill or any kind of safety drill, middle school excitability is high for hours thereafter.

- Safety regulations – How much are these practiced and promoted? Is safety such a big concern that everyone has a heightened sense of danger? Or, is there an ease about everyone's demeanor?

> "I've got to stop reading here for a moment because I am starting to get so overwhelmed and this list isn't over – not by a long shot!

Yup! It is pretty amazing just how many people and things come together for the purpose of your child's education on a daily basis. One way to deal with this overwhelming list of influences is to have a good dose of gratitude for all these things. Education is no small feat!

I want you as a parent to feel empowered as the champion of your child's educational experience. Please know that while it is important to understand all the influencing factors of your child's daily life, it is also equally important to understand that these influences converge at your child's school for education...*your* child's education. So, it all can be good! Even a difficult person or a power outage can be learning experiences. I will suggest ways at the end of this list how to be empowered as a parent. Please, keep reading!

School Location

- School campus – Is it landscaped nicely? Is it maintained for beauty? Is it utilized for education? Are there outdoor classrooms? Are there picnic tables in good condition?

- School perimeter – Is there a fence to establish the school border so that kids know where to be? Is it in good condition? Can anyone get on the campus? Do students know to keep perimeter fencing locked?

- Surrounding land – What is the area surrounding the school campus? Is it aesthetically pleasing? What message does it convey?

Community

- Observers from other schools – Often administration from other middle schools observe other settings. Are they observing with appreciation or judgment?

- Guest speakers – Was the topic agreeable with your child? Was the guest speaker interesting? Non-middle school people sometimes don't know how to talk to middle school kids and can become a source of irritation.

- PTA parents – These parents can offer much assistance to the school in many ways, such as providing supplies, parent communication, positive teacher morale, and fundraiser opportunities, and they can play favoritism, can judge other students and teachers, and can be part of negative school politics. Ask about being on the PTA board and watch the reaction closely. This will tell you much.

- Local community – The relationship between a school and its community is really important. This relationship translates into support or criticism from microphones everywhere, for example, church pulpits, volunteer/charity clubs, and public events. What does your child's school do to promote positive community relationships? Does your child's school have business partners?

Politics

- Mayor – What is the mayor's educational agenda? Evidence of this appears in the classroom. Does this person promote positive relations with schools? Do students know that this person supports them?

- School Board Members – What is the school board's educational agenda? Evidence of this appears in the classroom. Do students know that all school board members support them?

- District administration – What is the district administration's educational agenda? Evidence of this appears in the classroom. Do students know that all of the district administrators support them?

- District administration and its relationship with the principal – Has the district put more demands on the principal than the principal can easily manage? Is the principal friendly, relaxed, and unperturbed, or tensed, stressed, and overwhelmed? The principal's disposition permeates throughout the school to every student.

- State representatives – What is the state educational agenda? Evidence of this appears in the classroom. Do students know that the state leaders support them?

- President of the United States – What is the president's educational agenda? Evidence of this appears in the classroom. Do students know that the president supports them?

- News media – How does the local media portray your child's school and district? Is it favorable? Are they present for every negative incident, but rarely there for the positive events?

- World, nation, state, and city economics – School budgets quickly and directly reflect economic status at each of these levels. Does your child's school have what it needs? What it wants? Does your child see abundance or scarcity at school?

- Political climate – Students at this age are aware of politics and the effect they can have on the world to inside their homes. How are politics discussed in your home? At school? How much does this affect your child's disposition? The political climate can bring about positive or negative changes in schools.

Miscellaneous

- Regional geography – Do you live in a rainy, snowy, arid, or windy area? Do you live near water, mountains, flatlands, or hills? Does this agree with your child?

- Your child's overall health – Is your child affected by monthly menstrual cycles? Is your child affected by seasonal allergies? Is your child affected by mold, dust, rust, parasites, certain food ingredients, cleaning products, chalk dust, or other common products associated with being in public schools?

- Community population – Sudden building expansions create issues for schools. The dynamics of a school can dramatically change (for the better, of course!) when multiple new homes appear.

- School consolidations – For many reasons, districts may decide to consolidate schools. This totally transforms affected schools for a few years after the consolidation.

- Time of the day – Is your child a morning person or a night owl? Is your child slow to start in the morning? Does your child get tired after lunch? Does your child become overly excitable at a certain time? What subjects does your child have before or after lunch, first or last? The last period of the day tends to get cut short for many school reasons such as returning back to homerooms for progress report distribution.

- Uniforms – The pros and cons of school uniforms affect students. Some like it; some do not. What are the uniform requirements and how is this monitored?

- Number of clubs, activities, and morale boosting events such as pep rallies – Keep 'em busy! Middle school kids love to be involved, take part in school related activities, and have lots of fun! What is available for your child?

- Emotional and spiritual school climate – It is quite easy to sense a school's spirit upon entering. Do students feel good about being at school? Do they know they are in a successful school or a struggling school? What are the expectations of students and are they empowered by leadership opportunities? This will all be very evident, because if it exists, you will sense it and there will be pictures, trophies, and other displays proving such. For a parent, this will translate into you being excited about your child going to the school.

- Volunteers/classroom parents – These folks can be very helpful, can greatly assist, can play favoritism, can judge other students or teachers, and can be irritating.

- Weather – It is all around us 24-7 so it is an influencing factor for your child as well. How does weather affect your child? What is your child's favorite weather? Does your child have any weather fears? Do you have an emergency plan in place for severe weather? Expect stories on rainy days…it's almost guaranteed!

- Female menstrual cycles – All females react differently during their particular "time of the month." How many teachers are female? How many students are female? How many support staff are female? You get the picture, right?

- Time of the year – Is it close to the end of the year? Everyone gets anxious, worn out, and moody. And, I mean everyone!

> "Whew! Glad that list is over! That was a loooong list of influences. There are so many ones I hadn't thought about as having an impact on my child on a daily basis. I can see how each one has an influence with wide ranging variance. Wow. Thank you for providing much for me to consider if my child comes home after a bad day. But, I am feeling drained right now. It is as if there are too many influences affecting my child. How do I deal with so many? How does my *child* deal with so many?"

Yes. You are right. It is quite a list. It overwhelms those working inside the building too. The point of the list for parents is to keep the influencing variables in mind when handling situations that arise with your middle school child. Who and what else was involved with a situation? Where and when was the situation? Try to obtain the whole picture before addressing any issues because it is not just about the teachers.

Part of the reason you feel drained is because many of them you cannot control, or so it seems that you cannot control them. Weather? Politics? How does a parent protect a child or control those variables of the middle school environment? A parent can begin the empowerment process by thinking that protection is not needed.

> "Um...what? My child *always* needs protection! The long list you wrote – it is all about all the influencing factors on my child. Of course, my child needs protection!"

Empower yourself and your child to the point that protection is not needed, but understood or assumed. Feel the difference between needed and assumed? One says, "I am scared," while the other one says, "All is well." Yes, there are influences all around us all the time. This is the great diversity of life! Yippie for influencing factors of life! These very things can be wonderful aspects of life or not. The people and things listed in this chapter can be positive contributors to life or not. Which will you choose for yourself and thus encourage your child to choose?

For example, weather. We obviously cannot control it. What can one do, then? A student can embrace the current weather conditions, wear the appropriate outerwear for it, and find the opportunities in the weather, such as sloshing in mud puddles, sliding down snow mounds, or listening to rain "music" on the roof. A mean school nurse. Students can see it as a fun challenge to get him or her to smile, while acknowledging the ill-tempered person's attitude has nothing to do with them. Small school budget. A student (or parent) can be creative with what funds have been provided for the school and ponder ways to create more money for the school. Many, wonderful, and profitable ideas have come from a place of desire for more! Unsightly neighborhood surrounding the school. There are many opportunities with this one! Students may brainstorm ideas, gather community support, and earn volunteer hours by beautifying the neighborhood. The sense of accomplishment will be something the students take with them waaaaay into adulthood. President's educational agenda. If this appears to be out of balance with what feels good to students, then this is opportunity to complete what is missing from the education agenda. In other words, if the president declares that all middle school students must take a foreign language, but reduces accelerated math courses, then embrace the foreign language class while continuing higher level math learning at the local college, from a tutor, or with an on line program. Class bully. This influencing factor is pretty clear cut: be bullied or befriend. How can one befriend a bully while maintaining one's own dignity, or keeping a balance between the two students? Opportunity abounds with many options such as inviting the child and/or child's family to your house for dinner, investigating what is feeding the bullying (Is the bully neglected at home?), and gathering resources like a guidance counselor to assist easing the negative interactions. In this situation, both students need to wear invisible signs that permanently adhere to their chests that say,"I am confident just with me."

Are any of the influences problems? Only if one views them as such. Pre-pave your child's way through the long list of middle school influences by creating a vibe of,"I'm already awesome," and,"I am confidently safe." The list will then not seem so daunting. Most perceived bad things do not happen because people are simply not aware of what could happen in the first place! Send your child to school already knowing and understanding that he or she is completely safe, and that all situations are merely opportunities.

You Are Now an Empowered Parent

Now you are empowered with this knowledge to be in a position to see the whole, big school picture to assist your child with daily situations. Now you are empowered to choose between needing protection and already knowing it is there, *and* to share this power with your child. You are empowered to see any supposed negative influencing factor as opportunity. You have been empowered to choose to live the life you want for yourself and for your child despite any situation. The empowerment comes from the realization that you are not trapped at all, you are not confined no matter what appears to be negative in your life, and you are not stuck in a situation with no options. Rather, empowerment comes from knowing, understanding, and assuming that situations will always be there to support you, are mere opportunities to seek solutions from the vast selection of options, and are sources of tremendous personal growth. Be empowered to live a great life and empower your child to enter the doors of middle school knowing, understanding, and assuming the same!

EIGHT

The First Year in Middle School

This chapter targets the year after your child completes elementary school and moves to the next academic step. In this book, I label the first year as sixth grade, the next year as seventh grade, and the last year as eighth grade, while recognizing that the number attached to these grades may vary depending on your school system. No matter the label, the first year is a very special year, indeed! It is characterized as the year your young one grows up…A LOT. Your child will not completely mature, thankfully, but you will notice a huge change. Sixth graders come in so "green." Expect a transformational year—for the better, of course!

The beginning of the year can be overwhelming for your child. Thus, you have a really good reason to do at least some of the suggestions mentioned previously in this book, including starting the positive lists about middle school. There will be more teachers, more teaching styles, more transitions, more places to lose personal items, lockers, lock combinations, clothing changes for P.E., more socialization opportunities, more clubs and after-school activities, more and higher level school work, yet fewer breaks during the day than elementary school. All of these changes need an adjustment period. The duration of the adjustment period varies from student to student. Although sixth grade teachers tend to have extra nurturing abilities, they still desire, however, that students make those adjustments sooner rather than later.

Generally, middle school teachers are not as "warm and fuzzy" as elementary school teachers. Of the three middle school teaching levels, sixth grade teachers usually are the most nurturing. They welcome, assist, care for, organize, and encourage sixth grade students for longer and to a greater degree than the rest. The other teachers *thank* sixth grade teachers for preparing the students for seventh and eighth grades! If done well, sixth grade teachers provide a magnificent start to a wonderful, amazing, successful, and thrilling middle school experience. By the end of the year, the sixth grade students are much more independent and organized. They have a solid understanding of how middle school functions. They are involved in school activities and are ready to take on more leadership in the school. It truly is a transformational year!

> "Before you go further, I would like to know more about the differences between middle school teachers and elementary school teachers. I can sense the difference just by interacting with them, but what exactly are the differences?"

Good question! Teachers seem to find their places where they belong in the vast array of teaching opportunities. There is great diversity even within the walls of one school. A teacher having a good time in kindergarten may not be as successful teaching fourth grade because he or she is best suited to interact with really young children. Some teachers want more nurturing opportunities while some want more curriculum focused opportunities. Some have tolerance for organized chaos while others desire order. There are teachers who are inclined to be elementary school teachers because they easily display those characteristics just as there are teachers who are inclined to be middle school teachers because they easily display those characteristics.

Over all, middle school teachers tend to speak direct. Middle school students are addressed more like adults now. The high pitched voices of elementary teachers are replaced with lower voices. The mindset has changed from one hundred percent assisting to partially assisting. The message is "Get yourself together," as the ball is thrown in the child's court. More responsibility is asked of middle school students. Late work may not be accepted. There may be fewer smiles, stickers, and hugs, but these are replaced with more verbal praises and pats on the back, as teacher to student physical touching moves to the extremities, such as high fives and handshakes.

At first, these differences can seem unfeeling, but within a month or two, your child adjusts and realizes that he does not need the stickers, the warm fuzzies, or the constant monitoring anymore. Your child now grasps that she can monitor herself, make herself feel good, and focus on higher level learning. As she transitions the first year, turn any complaints around to positive statements so that your child can see how well she is adapting to the new academic environment. What successes are already present? Did she get a good grade? Did she stay calmer today? Did she remember her locker combination today? Did she make a new friend this week? Did the teacher smile with a joke your child shared? Did your child go beyond the assignment and was acknowledged? Find whatever you can that is positive and build from that point.

I always told my seventh grade students to allow themselves two weeks for adjusting to the school year beginning. By stating it this way, the allowance was a gift they could give to themselves. Sixth graders, most likely, will need more than two weeks. Take a look at the compiled middle school skills and estimate which ones are new for your child. How many of these will be a thrilling and successful challenge for your child?

Teachers:

- Adapt to up to six or more teaching styles, personalities, and pet peeves
- Engage teachers after class about grades and assignments
- Reduce reliance on teacher's monitoring
- Proactively recognize and verbalize needs

Building:

- Manage space at lockers with multiple peers in close proximity
- Memorize a lock combination and how to use it
- Learn the hallway movement pattern
- Learn the location of six or more teachers
- Evaluate the best route to classes

Personal Development:

- Determine and pursue school involvement
- Monitor own emotional health
- Persevere on a "bad day" without requiring much consoling from another
- Persist finding positive qualities in peers, teachers, and/or subjects found to be irritating
- Evaluate and utilize additional resources such as the media specialist

- Monitor time for personal needs such as bathroom and drink breaks

- Learn time management to arrive punctually with required supplies

- Postpone dealing with a conflict to concentrate on school lessons

Peer Interactions:

- Navigate through an oncoming sea of students

- Positively interact with upper grade students

- Cooperate with many different peer personalities, ethnic backgrounds, and social groups

- Choose personal peer group

- Assess dependable friends

Academics:

- Discover one's own learning style, note-taking style, and studying style

- Discover one's own mental break style, such as doodling or stretching

- Prepare for and carry two or three classes' supplies for a period of time

- Participate in classroom discussions, activities, and assignments more

- Rise up to the challenge of each subject and this year's academic increase

- Maintain organized notebooks

- Log daily, weekly, and monthly academics in an agenda
- Focus for longer periods of time on one subject
- Remember the requirements of each class

> "Wow! That is a lot! I'm amazed how students do this year after year in sixth grade. What a change from elementary school. No wonder middle school is scary."

It is only scary if you believe it to be. Middle school is an exhilarating challenge; one that can be wonderful, awesome, successful, and thrilling with a focus of these things! Yes, there may be times when it feels scary. With an adjustment, the scariness goes away and is replaced with wonder, awe, success, and thrill. Why do some people do "scary" things like climb really tall mountains such as Mt. Everest? It is for the wonder, awe, and thrill of success! Middle school can be your child's Mt. Everest (and yours too). Climbers prepare backpacks, collect supplies, and focus thoughts before one foot is set on the mountain. This book is helping you do the same for your child – prepare, collect, and focus!

If your child is still struggling after two weeks, seek teacher input. Some students need more assistance than others. This is normal. The point is to get your child to independence eventually, right? There is no incorrect path to achieve this goal. Teachers will be an invaluable resource for your child.

~

Seeing the Connection Between Classroom and Career

Sixth grade is a great time to start discussions about career possibilities, if you haven't done so already. Allow your child to visit people in their careers at various times during the year. You possibly could get these days counted as school days with prior approval from the principal. Ask your school to participate in The Job Shadow Coalition program.[10] It is usually held on Ground Hog's Day, February 2. See, the legend is that on February 2 of every year, if the groundhog sees its shadow…OK, you get the connection.

Arrange a job shadowing experience on a teacher workday, teacher professional development day, or a holiday when school is not in session. Veterinarians, doctors, lawyers, businesses, law enforcement workers, hospitals, and others, work on these special school calendar days. Job shadowing days must be planned way in advance with prior permission, as much preparation takes place to accommodate a student observer. Lawyers must plan the day's activities to not include private information for client-representative privileges to remain intact. Doctors must obtain prior written permission from patients about having a student observer present and plan which nurse will be in charge of the student. Veterinarians may prefer to have a student observer on surgery days instead of patient days. They'll need to have an extra surgical outfit ready. Even though planning for student observers requires extra work, it is widely welcomed in most work places as adults enjoy teaching about their jobs to the young. There is something natural, almost a-granola-crunchy-earth-loving-innate desire to show the young how to do a job, and the preparation effort is worth the joy of sharing.

I have included this subject in the sixth grade year because at some time during this transformational year, these students "get it" that they are growing up and want to understand the connection between the classroom and real life. When students have this understanding or have ambition to join a certain career, much argument for what is academically required in middle school can be eliminated. They almost embrace the academic challenges! So, how about your own workplace for job shadowing? Two things may happen:

1. Your child may learn with more ease about your job since your child has probably heard you talk about your job a lot more than other jobs—due to close proximately to the worker (you!). She will be able to understand the classroom to career

connection much quicker than if it is a field of which she has no prior knowledge.

2. Your child may have a whole new respect for you. Ever come home tired and your child does not really care? Ever come home exhausted and your child wants you to drive him to the mall? You say no, but he whines until you do? If he experiences what you do during the day, he may offer to make you dinner that night!

There could be multiple benefits to taking your child to your workplace. The educational value of such a day is vast and can bring meaning to what is taught in the classroom.

To establish this program as a regular middle school offering at your child's school, explain to the principal the multiple benefits of this program. She can use the program as bragging rights to the community. I worked with a principal who loved Job Shadowing Day. Declaring that ninety-seven percent of the student body participated in job shadowing on a particular day is impressive. It reflected much about the quality of the school. Students had "buy in" with job shadowing. Parents arranged transportation. Guidance counselors created registration and completion papers, talked to each homeroom about the purpose, requirements, and desired manners in the work place, and collected the paperwork from each student who desired to participate *prior and after* the job shadowing day. Teachers planned for this event before (avoid tests and major note taking on this day), during (for the three percent at school), and after (reports and presentations about job shadowing experiences). A successful school's job shadowing experience is also reflective of the school's relationship with the community. Businesses will say yes much quicker if the school has previously reached out to its community rather than if the school has not. Discuss job shadowing to all of your child's teachers, guidance counselor(s), and parents. How about the PTA? Pretty soon your child's school will be embracing job shadowing as a part of the regular curriculum!

Elementary school students' primary focus was the "here and now." It was getting good grades, participating in school activities, and enjoying life. Once children enter middle school, the focus shifts to how the "here and now" relates to their futures. It is a slight change, but a very important one, thus the reason to ensure career observation opportunities for your child.

~

Extra-curricular Activities, Relationships, and Diversity

Awesome middle schools offer many more extra-curricular opportunities than elementary schools for very good reasons. Encourage involvement with your child for several reasons:

- Discovering one's talents and interests
- Creating avenues for friendships
- Cultivating self-esteem
- Learning time management (both activities and homework are completed)
- Developing decision making strategies (Which opportunities will I pick?)
- Exploring the diversity of life
- And, the #1 reason to encourage involvement is...involved and engaged middle school students are happier kids!

Want to live with a happy middle school student? Get your sixth grader involved with extra-curricular activities. Engaged kids tend to stay out of trouble, earn better grades, and have healthier relationships. This may mean more commitment from you. How will your child get home from an after school meeting? How will your child get to a basketball game on the other side of town Saturday morning? It is all worth the effort because your child is now having a wonderful, awesome, successful, and thrilling middle school experience!

Middle school offers many more social opportunities too. Sixth grade may be the first time your child (and, therefore, you too) experience these new and different social outlets. Boy-girl parties, electronic communication with both boys and girls, and school dances are all part of the middle school experience.

It is always quite noticeable in middle school hallways, even to the uninterested observer, the wide range of student heights. This tremendous variance is quite pronounced in sixth grade. Students have their growth spurts at different times and the result is students who look almost adult beside students who look like they snuck into middle school before finishing fourth grade. It is a great opportunity to celebrate diversity because that is exactly what it is! Sixth grade students tend to remain fairly constant with their clothing styles and hairstyles – meaning they do not change these often. How they looked and what they wore at the beginning of sixth grade is most likely to be similar at the end of sixth grade. Facial breakouts and body odors may be issues this year. If they are concerns, please address the situations quickly, sympathetically, and privately. Females may begin their menstrual cycles this year, if not already. Again, quick, sympathetic, and private guidance will be most appreciative. Need to shop for personal undergarments such as a bra? Marvel with your child how his or her body is developing perfectly according to his or her own specific schedule, and assure that all physical development will be complete soon. Embracing the diversity—tall or short, menstrual cycle or not, blemishes or not, body odor or not—will help diminish any awkwardness about these bodily changes.

Yes, sixth grade is a transformational year for your child. It will certainly be time to celebrate when the year is complete. Utilize the positive lists about sixth grade to record successes. Turn any perceived negatives into positive learning experiences. Reflect on friendships made, organizational skills accumulated, time management efforts improved, and those "mysterious," sometimes puzzling teacher pet-peeves conquered!

NINE

The "Middle of the Middle" Year

Uh oh! It is the "middle of the middle" year. Hold on to your hats! Expect an interesting seventh grade year…in a good way, of course!

If there is a year you will need to implement a "stay focused on your child, but give them space" system, this will probably be the year. Bewildered, parents come in for conferences with worn out expressions on their faces. It is as if they have lost something very important to them. In response to their forlorn looks and to assure them this is somewhat normal, I have told this short, humorous story to many parents over the years:

> An alien has come to Earth and has taken your child away. Inside the body of what looks like your child is really an alien. Your child will be returned in a year or two. Just love the alien and look forward to your child coming back sooner than later.

However strange the story, it did relieve parents, as I have observed this pattern repeat, especially with male students. I have seen children change back to themselves as quickly as by the next year in eighth grade. When I would see the positive change in them and jokingly ask why they were not like that last year in seventh grade when I was teaching them, they sorta just shrug their shoulders and grin a mischievous smile filled with wonderful moments of adventure as memories come rushing back. Then, a maturity grin replaces the mischievous smile knowing that they have in fact matured and they like it. Then, they would utter, "I dunno."

Yup! My alien story must be true!

Parental strategy is essential for this year. Rev up your engines and prepare your positive strategies ahead of time. Really focus on what works well for your child with a good dosage of flexibility.

> "Is the seventh grade year tough for every student? What makes this year so challenging? My next door neighbor's daughter is in seventh grade this year and she seems fine. My sister's son enjoyed his seventh grade year!"

Just like with anything in life, you will find those who succeed in troubling times and those who will fail in good times. Just like with anything in life, you will find the contrary to any declaration ever stated! It is my observation of students and parents during the eight years I taught seventh grade, that this year is more likely to be a year of challenging, testing, proving, defining, maturing, and growing than the sixth grade year or the eighth grade year. There were many exceptions to this statement and many who absolutely loved their seventh grade years!

Do you know anyone who is the middle child? Do you know the common traits and behaviors associated with the middle child? Of course, many exceptions to these generalities exist. Being the middle child does not automatically mean you are going to feel neglected in your family. I am providing strategies that can be utilized whenever they are needed.

Seventh grade is the year to do lots of talking with your child about the changes in her world. Discuss the many choices to handle those changes. Plan this communication time daily because of the possible intensity of this year. I routinely ask three questions of my daughter at bedtime: How are you feeling? (Wait for honest, thoughtful answer.) Is there anything bothering you? (Wait for reflection time.) Is there anything you want to talk about? (Assure that you are there for her or him no matter what happens anywhere anytime independent of the severity of the issue.) The end of the day seemed the best time for us to discuss things. It was when "problems" or things that bothered her had opportunity to be brought forth because the business of the day was gone. I have had some of the best talks with her at bedtime! When issues surface, show your child that many, many options exist for any situation and that she is never stuck, caught in a bind, or powerless. Explain she is the positive creator of her life!

~

Empowerment Through Acknowledging All Options

Your child is involved with the school chorus and was not picked for a solo as expected. Your child is upset. Assisting your child to list all of his possible options (and I do mean all of them!), discussing the outcomes of each one, and empowering your child to choose an option or several options that he deems will suit him best is valuable and empowering!

So, possible options for his scenario are:

- Cry
- Yell
- Tell the other kid he got it for a reason other than talent
- Quit chorus

- Sing poorly from now on
- Be sarcastic toward the teacher
- Break something in anger
- Break a designated object in anger
- Feel rejected
- Act mad in chorus from now on
- Tell others how unfair the selection was
- Talk about the person who was selected
- Write a hostile letter to the teacher
- Write an honest letter to the teacher
- Talk to the teacher about what happened and learn why not picked
- Do self-analysis for why not picked
- Take voice lessons from a person outside of the school
- Practice more
- Research audition techniques
- Focus on other opportunities available for the vocal talent
- Evaluate what thoughts were present before and during the audition—were they focused on obtaining the part or on the competitor getting the part?

- Align energy, focus, and thoughts on own personal desires with lots of powerful, positive feeling to bring forth the desired results when the next opportunity arises

Wow! What a list of options! Do you think your child now would feel disempowered or empowered? He now gets to choose what he wants to do! It may be that the child in this scenario decides to implement the options of yell, write a hostile letter to the teacher, and take voice lessons from a person not associated with the school.

> "Some of those options are rather negative. Are you suggesting that children utilize angry options? I want my children to be well-behaved and to accept disappointment calmly, respectfully, and properly. I like the ones at the bottom of the list better than the ones at the top of the list. Please explain."

The point of the complete list of all possible options is to validate how a child feels about a situation. The way a child feels is the way a child feels. Children get angry when their feelings are ignored, judged, shunned, or dismissed. The list empowers a child to view all possible options, acknowledge that expressing anger is an option even if not a positive one, evaluate which ones will produce the results the child desires, and feel empowered in the selection process. As anger is acknowledged, it diminishes in importance. Empowerment replaces anger since the child embraces the freedom of choosing options. With proper parental guidance, a child can choose options that produce what he truly wants. Does he truly want revenge? No. Does he truly want to be mean? No. What he truly wants is to be accepted, understood, respected, and successful. When empowered and focused on his true desires, a child will choose the options that obtain those things for him.

The child in the scenario feels angry and frustrated because he believes he cannot have what he wants, when in reality, he can have everything he wants. By the power of his focus (only on his true desires), he will become a strong magnet and attract them through this or other avenues. The list of possible options allows him to see which options will bring about his true desires.

> "You wrote the child in the scenario chose yelling, writing a hostile letter to the teacher, and taking voice lessons. Only one of the three options is positive. The other two options are disrespectful and aggressive. I cannot support this! Where is all the positive thinking and energy you wrote about so much in previous chapters?"

I love your question! All the positive thinking and energy is right in the middle of empowerment! Take a look at the options again. The child can utilize options to release his frustration and anger such as yelling, breaking something, or crying. He can then choose the options that focus on what he really wants such as voice lessons, talking to the teacher, and evaluating the thoughts he was having before and during the audition to ensure success next time!

> "Breaking something? That's a positive option? You've got to be kidding!"

Fortunately, I am not kidding. Kids around the world are cheering! No, I am not a proponent of violence in any way in any manner at anytime. One reason humans act violently toward others, things, or themselves is because the normal, natural human emotion of anger is ignored, judged, shunned, or dismissed. There are many, many nonhurtful, wonderful ways to release angry feelings!

Just having those options on the list is empowering. The goal is to transfer angry feelings to empowerment feelings. Listing breaking objects as an option does just that. Of course, you will guide your child from actually doing that option because it can be harmful in many ways and will not produce the desired end result. Some children do need a physical release of the tension created from their anger. In this case there are many options, one of which is to break or rip apart a family-designated object such as a cardboard box, an old ready-to-be-thrown-out electronic device, old t-shirts, sticks, or used pencils.

> "You like the word *options*, don't you? I'm still not buying the idea of negative choices as positive responses to disappointment. Why do you believe that yelling and writing an angry letter to the teacher are positive options?"

The child in the chorus scenario chose to yell as a positive option to release his anger. Yelling does not always have to be done toward others. Sometimes I yell, scream, or groan as loud as I can when alone in my house. And, you know what? It feels great!! I can physically feel the tension leaving my body. Sometimes, I yell, scream, and groan until I start to laugh. The release of negative emotions feels so good I start laughing! Crying has the same effect. Some people begin laughing after crying. Why? Crying is the world's best releaser of negative emotion. After it is released, some feel like celebrating.

~

The Benefits of an Anger Pillow

In my classroom, I had an anger pillow. It was always available for any child at any time. It was taken into the hallway or outside. The child either yelled into the pillow to release anger, or the child yelled while smashing the pillow on the wall, beam, outside bricks, or floor to release anger. It was never used on another human being or another object that could break. I declare this: ninety-nine percent of the time, the child was smiling before he or she made it out of my classroom with the pillow! Just the thought of yelling into a pillow and being given permission to smash a pillow onto a school wall made most of my students release anger in less than thirty seconds! I strongly suggest every household have an anger pillow.

The child in chorus also selected writing a hostile letter to the teacher as another option to release anger. The purpose is to honor those intense feelings so he will not give the letter to the teacher, but gosh, it sure feels good to express those angry feelings on paper.

The last option the child chose was to take voice lessons. With this choice, the child positively makes a committed decision to be the best singer he can be. Taking voice lessons requires practice and time. Perhaps, he thought a voice teacher could teach him audition skills too. Hopefully, these three chosen options will assist the child to be successful with the next audition. If not, then the list of possible choices is still available to him.

Empowering your child to choose from the variety of options is the best gift you can offer any year in middle school, but especially during the seventh grade year. Communication is key to soothe the seventh grade year and ensure that a wonderful, awesome, successful, and thrilling middle school experience continues.

> "So, it is the having of choices that really gives the empowerment to my child. This way he won't feel so blocked in by the situation once he sees the long list of options available to him. I can guide him to those options that will bring emotional release *and* offer power to deal with a difficult situation. Now, I get it!"

Yes! It is really a two-part method!

~

Middle School Intermittent "Breaks"

Another helpful strategy with the "middle of the middle" year is allowing your child more breaks than you normally would, including more job shadowing opportunities than just the one time on February 2. If seventh grade is a year of challenging what is, then allow more opportunities to see how school curriculum relates to the work force. Instead of once a year, how about once a quarter? Assuming grades and behavior are in check, this might just be one strategy to help your child (and you) through this year.

In addition, having lunch with your child on and off campus in another strategy. Nothing smells of freedom and good vibes than being taken away from the school campus for a lunch at a favorite fast food restaurant. Make it quick, as most middle school lunch schedules are tightly adhered…about thirty minutes. Resist the ensuing pleas to keep her out for the rest of the day. Bring lunch to the school. You can stay or not. It is the freedom factor and the "coolness" factor you provide. Also, by doing so, you raise your own "coolness" level too… with your child and your child's peers. That's so cool!

Surprises keep the positive attention of your seventh grader. Depending on your child's personality, how about the following suggestions?

- Send a flower, balloon, or teddy bear bouquet to your daughter at school *not* on Valentine's Day, (Know your child…the embarrassment could backfire on you. On the other hand, some extroverts would *love* this attention.)

- Slip a crisp, new twenty dollar bill into your child's nighttime reading just because.

- Go on a surprise ski trip to the mountains for a long weekend (Thursday to Monday).

- Plan a surprise trip to NYC, Montreal, San Francisco, Atlanta, or Denver

- Write about a future surprise you have planned in your child's school agenda.

- Keep your child home a day to complete school projects, if necessary.

- Plan your child's favorite dinner.

Retrieve your child early from school to do something fun:

- Walk in a wooded area or on the beach together

- Do a surprise shopping trip

- Get manicures or pedicures, have hair done, or get ears pierced

- Ride go carts at a local theme park

- Throw a ball with your child and dog at the park

- Feed ducks or geese at a pond

- Go swimming, play tennis, or shoot hoops

- Spend hours at the bookstore

- Get ice cream

- Create and/or paint pottery

- Play video games or watch a movie

Your child will be ever so thankful for these breaks and surprises, and you might see an ease with this year. Make them rare, but often enough to relieve the potential tension of the seventh grade year. These opportunities give your child a break, if needed, and give you an opportunity to bond and talk with your child. Doing these special events with your child enables you to have more of your child's attention. Of course, if your child is sailing though seventh grade with a song in her heart, these strategies may or may not be necessary. You can do them another time if your child is struggling or do them just because!

> "It sounds like you are encouraging time away from school—more than the allotted holidays as stated by the district school calendar."

I am not promoting cutting school, playing hooky, truancy, or preventing perfect school attendance with these suggestions. School is very important and being present as much as possible is extremely beneficial to academic success. However, if your middle school child is not enjoying school, having a difficult year, or struggling with some aspect of middle school, how much of your child is actually mentally present, although physically present at school? Intermittent breaks have much value if used to promote a wonderful, awesome, successful, and thrilling middle school experience.

~

Physical Growth, Relationships, and Academics

Of course, seventh grade students continue to mature physically. The wide range of student heights narrows a bit. Some will have hit their growth spurts and look like skyscrapers, while there will still be a few students who are the same size as those in elementary school, but not as many as last year. In exchange, "Mt. Vesuvius" (a.k.a. zits or pimples), blemishes, acne, body odors of all types, creative hairstyles, and attention getting clothing become pronounced this year. If you have not already, you may be asked to purchase creams, cover ups, concealers, special cleansers, deodorant, body sprays, perfume, hair accessories, jewelry, "loud" clothing, shirts with attitude messages and/or images, brand name sneakers, multiple shoes, and many appointments at the hairdresser for your child. If personal hygiene has not already become very important to your child, please, for everyone's sake, plan to have a discussion immediately! Personal hygiene products are a must for all students this age and especially for those taking physical education classes. Go with your child and have fun selecting products from the vast choices. Purchase an extra set for school.

Students keep these hygiene products in their lockers (homeroom and gym lockers) or purses and can reapply during breaks, if needed.

Friendships remain important and are in more focused groups. After the transformational year in sixth grade, student friendships settle into friend clusters. Seventh grade students' personalities become more defined and this is reflected in "hanging out" with similar personalities. Girl and boy interactions increase with the same defining process of what they like and do not like in crushes. Seventh grade students may want to socialize independent of parents. They will want to meet friends at public places, such as the mall or movie theater. Know your child's ability to handle these types of situations or not, be aware of who will be with your child, get to know these other students and the students' parents, know exactly where your child will be the whole time, give your child a way to communicate with you for the entire time, make periodic contacts with each other, and teach your child what to do for all scenarios in public places, as there will be students from other schools at the mall or movie theater as well.

Seventh grade academics will be pushed up a notch or two. I always heard every year, at the beginning of the school year, groans and complaints about how much harder seventh grade was and how mean we all were and how much more work there was and how much they wanted to go back to sixth grade when the teachers were nice and on and on the groaning and complaining went…until it stopped… somewhere around Thanksgiving. At the same time, I always received visits by eighth grade students who groaned and complained to me about how much harder eighth grade was and how mean the eighth grade teachers were and how much more work there was and how much they wanted to go back to seventh grade so I could be their teacher again when the work was easy and on and on continued the groaning, complaining, and visits …until they stopped… somewhere around Thanksgiving.

I bet a ninth grade teacher at the high school is hearing from those ninth grade students about how….

TEN

The Last Year in Middle School

Ah! You and your child finally made it to eighth grade. It is time to relax, right? WRONG! While your child may have matured since last year and may take his academics more seriously, there is much to do this year to get ready for high school. The middle school guidance counselor will be working with eighth grade students from the start of the year for this important preparation.

Two things:

1. Make sure you and your child know the high school enrollment requirements and if she has successfully completed all required credits for high school.

2. Make sure your child is submitting his or her best possible work now in eighth grade for the highest positive academic placement in high school courses.

Appropriate and positive academic placement in high school is essential for a confident start. Proving oneself after ninth grade has begun is much more difficult than proving oneself in eighth grade and receiving the proper placement in high school that comes as a reward from successful academic achievement. It would be much better for your child to start his high school experience with the group of people who are academic-minded and will be his peers for the duration of the high school experience. The eighth grade teachers understand this and also desire to make the transition to high school for students as easy as possible. The eighth grade teachers' focus will be on creating a bridge to high school, so academics will be augmented once again.

Begin now researching what the high school offers in every aspect, just like you did for the beginning of middle school. What sports, clubs, activities, related arts, and special courses are offered? Does the high school have programs for opting out of final exams if a student's grades are high enough? Does the high school allow students to leave the campus early on certain days if all of their classes are completed? Does the high school offer specialized courses such as accelerated IB (International Baccalaureate) or AP (Advanced Placement) courses? Will the high school accept credits from other sources that could be taken during the summer? What are the high school's strengths? So, while it is time to enjoy all the fun of being an eighth grader in middle school, it is also time to focus on making high school a wonderful, awesome, successful, and thrilling experience too!

Reflect on the successes and challenges of the past years. Are there negative events still lingering that can be turned into something positive? What school skills and strategies worked for your child? Are there new strategies that will be beneficial for this year that would not have worked previously? How well do you know the eighth grade teacher personalities and what can you do to prepare for them?

Middle School Kings and Queens

The eighth graders are the oldest students of the building and this gives them an extra boost of confidence, as well as certain privileges *and* responsibilities. Privileges may come in the form of assisting in the front office, helping the day porter, delivering papers to homerooms, preparing for and assisting with field day activities, being first to participate in school-wide events, partaking in eighth grade only activities, being the star players on sports teams, giving more input for school schedules and activities, conducting school tours for visitors, leading school clubs, making daily announcements, and standing guard at dismissal. Responsibilities may be established as setting the example for positive behavior, having the best grade point average of the school, raising the most money for school charity events, and welcoming/mentoring the incoming sixth grade class. With a few exceptions, the eighth graders embrace being "queens and kings" of the school and all that goes with these titles.

Most of the students have grown tremendously in height since sixth grade, so there is more uniformity with the class. Their bodies are showing definite signs of approaching adulthood as male facial hair may appear. Facial blemishes may still cause much concern for eighth graders. Many have calmed down into serious academically-oriented students and confident personalities, yet remain middle school silly. Clothing and hair styles, personal hygiene, friends, boy/girlfriends, and socialization are all very important. Often, schools have eighth grade formal dances near the end of the year—an event of great significance. You may notice more coupling with boys and girls this year mixed with break-ups, mixed with new boy/girlfriends, mixed with break-ups, mixed with.... It is all part of the dating process!

Before you can blink, graduation practices are happening, graduation celebrations are being planned, and graduation pictures are snapping. What a wonderful milestone in your child's life! Hopefully, eighth grade was the best year ever to a three-year successful experience in middle school. Graduation is a magnificent time to ponder all the growth and positive changes in your child's life and yours. Were you able to focus your thinking, emotions, and energy in such a way to model for your child positive creation of your life? Were you able to adapt your schedule to accommodate the increased middle school activities? How long are the lists of positive middle school experiences for your child? What an awesome graduation celebration to read through those lists!

Your child will have much confidence to move on to the next chapter in his life now that he has just completed middle school. *Just completed? Just completed*??!! Not quite a satisfactory or suitable choice of verb! Hopefully, these are more exact: Thrived! Bloomed! Succeeded! Your child will exclaim, "High school, here I come!"

ELEVEN

One Additional Middle School Student Definition

In a previous chapter, "What Is a Middle Schooler Anyway?," I listed several possible definitions of middle school students. There is one more I would like to add. This definition applies to any human of any age:

Every child (or human being or parent) is perfect just the way he or she is.

> "Um…perfect? Have you met my child? Perfect? No way. I could share lots of stories that would be the exception this definition."

I mean it. Every child is perfect just as is. Yes, I know children cause messes. Adults cause messes too. It all is still perfect. Your discomfort with this definition might be that *your* definition of perfect differs from your *child's* definition. So, whose definition is right? Both.

> "Both? Huh? In my house, Mom, me, (or Dad) is always right. What I say goes. Once junior is on his own, then he can decide what is right or perfect for him. A household can't have two definitions of what's perfect!"

Well, how is it going? Do you have peace in your house? Is there an easy flow permeating your house? Probably not all the time. Do you like being told how to live your life from an outside source? Suppose you live in a covenanted neighborhood. There are restrictions and regulations for many aspects of living in this neighborhood. Mow your grass this often. Landscape your house to a certain money amount. Submit your house improvement plans through the Architectural Review Board for approval first. Bring in your trash can within twenty-four hours of garbage pickup day. Park only in your driveway—no street parking. Kid toys and/or any yard debris must be removed from lawns daily. Privacy fence style must be one of a few predetermined styles. Privacy fences must be within stated regulatory height. Privacy fences must be within the stated reduced height if property backs up to a body of water—wetlands, marsh, swamp, stream, river, pond, or lake with prior approval. Privacy fence must be preapproved prior to building fence. Regime fees are paid monthly. If late or delinquent, a $25/day fee will be collected. On and on it goes. How about when you get a letter or a phone call about a neighborhood covenant you broke? What about other areas of life such as a police ticket, a parking fine, a tax increase, or a surprise bank fee? What about honking and road rage from another? What about a new traffic light on your way to work, a route detour, or a new neighborhood right behind yours? In reality, no one desires to be told how to live life from an outside source. Kids are no different.

~

What Is, Is Perfect

The honest truth is we all want to be honored, appreciated, have peace surrounding us, create the life we want, believe we are perfect just the way we are, and just simply feel good all the time.

> "How can that exist in a family setting? Or, since this book is about middle school, how can that exist in a school setting? How can everyone's definition of what's perfect be allowed? That sounds scary and chaotic!"

The key to this is simple: what is, is perfect. Each and every significant and insignificant event in life brought you to this very moment in your life. Each and every event had meaning to varying degrees. Each and every event supported you in the process of being you. Each and every event gave you opportunity to be more, grow further, experience new things, appreciate life from a new perspective, and realize more than the moment just before it. What is imperfect about any of that? It sounds perfect to me. So the "good," the "bad," and the "in between" events were perfect. What is *your* perfect is *your* perfect. Your child's perfect is your child's perfect. With this new definition of perfect, can you see that whatever your child does is perfect? With this new understanding, what happens is perfect. It gives you or your child opportunity to be more, grow further, experience new things, appreciate life from a new perspective, and realize more than the moment just before it. That's perfect.

> "So...mistakes, mess ups, faults are perfect? Are you serious? You are trying to explain to me how these things are perfect? It is a whole new definition! I think I'll have to contemplate this a bit before I understand it, but right now I think you mean that because my child gained something from the mishap, it can be seen as perfect before, during, and after it happened. And because it was my child's mishap, and not mine, it is my child's definition of perfect rather than my definition of perfect."

Yes, you are on your way to understanding this! Here are other aspects to consider. Can you see the multiple benefits of this definition of perfect?

- It eliminates the conflict of who is right and who is wrong while it adds the benefit of learning from events.
- It frees you from being the enforcer while it adds a positive parent-child relationship of acceptance.
- It rids the need for judgment while it breathes in self-analysis and acknowledgement.
- It eliminates your child's dependency on your direction while it encourages your child's independence.
- It sends the wonderful message that we are all loved, we are all perfect just the way we are, and we are on this life journey together.

> "That has a nice feel to it...in fact, very nice. I'd rather not always have to be on the lookout, always having to be in charge, always having to point out why something is wrong. But, I'll still have to consider all of this more to fully grasp the concept. I like it enough to try to understand."

Parental control is an illusion. It is not real.

> "OK. Good vibes now gone. Parental control is an illusion? Come on!"

Unless you are physically forcing a child to do something (not EVER recommended unless keeping a child from harm), you do not make anyone do anything by parental control. Some parents think that they have control over their kids. Not so at all. Each and every time, the child makes a decision to comply with the request or not to comply. What is perceived as parental control is really the child making the decision to comply. A child who decides to comply often is labeled well-behaved or respectful and deemed controlled, but in reality she is not controlled at all. The child is making her own decisions each and every time!

For example: a child is asked to end playing an electronic devise game to give attention to adult visitors, grandma, or whomever. The child is simply making the decision to agree to the parental request because the child likes peace, happiness, cooperation, and joy. If the child agrees to comply with ending the game, he receives those things—peace, happiness, cooperation, and joy. It was not parental control that made the child end the game, but the desire for the peace, happiness, and cooperation.

A child may make the decision to earn good grades because he wants peace in his life, not because he was told to get straight As. Perhaps, he earned good grades because he likes the rewards that come with academic success. Maybe he really enjoys learning new things and loves the thrills from challenges. Your precious daughter may make the decision to wear the dress you suggested because you are throwing in an incentive and logical rationale for her to wear it. It may seem she simply complied, but in reality, she made the decision because she enjoys family happiness more than being stubborn. Another child may decide to take the garbage out because he likes cooperation and sees the benefit of everyone doing a part to keep the house clean, not because he was told to do so. Students who participate in sports know that the benefit of working out, running laps, and listening to the coach are worth the effort because it gets them what they want—to play the sport! These students follow the coach's directions and endure workouts because they love playing the sport much, much more. Compliance gets them what they truly want. All human beings of all ages make decisions daily to comply or not comply based on what feels best to them.

> "Gosh. You are really stretching the limits of my beliefs. I am OK with it, however, because you provide logical explanations. I just have to grapple with it a bit. If I understand you correctly, parental control is an illusion because we are all separate human beings with decision making abilities and that if someone complies with a request, it is because he made a personal decision toward that which feels best to him. Hopefully, what feels best are the good things in life such as peace, happiness, cooperation, and joy. And if someone doesn't comply, it is because disagreement feels best to them."

That is correct.

> "Why would disagreement feel best to a human being?"

Well, sometimes someone's perfect is disagreement. Sometimes disagreement feels the best because the request does not feel good. Martin Luther King, Jr., a 1960's civil liberties vigilant, disagreed that African Americans were judged by skin pigment. Rosa Parks, who is considered the first woman of the civil rights movement, disagreed that she had to surrender her bus seat to another with lighter skin. Thomas Edison, an American inventor, disagreed that only candles could provide light in the dark. Alexander Graham Bell, the inventor of the telephone, disagreed that people could verbally communicate face to face only. Henry Ford, founder of the Ford Motor Company, disagreed that cars were purchased only by the wealthy. Gandhi, a practitioner of nonviolence, disagreed that indigenous people could be ruled by a foreign country. Bill Gates, chairman of Microsoft, disagreed that computers could only be used for businesses and had to be extremely large. Everyone who disagreed with a request, or the "it is just the way things are" mentality, did so because they made a decision toward what felt best to them.

Disagreement comes from deep inside people because people's natural state is love. People naturally want the positive emotions of peace, joy, and happiness. I strongly suspect Martin Luther King, Jr.'s disagreement felt uplifting, freeing, and exuberant to him. When the emotions or physical reality does not exist in people's lives according to their personal definitions of perfect, disagreement can feel like peace, joy, and happiness.

So, putting both concepts together…everyone's definition of perfection is as unique as there are people living on this planet, and, sometimes, disagreement is a person's definition of perfect for a particular time or topic.

> "Then, this has huge implications for all aspects of middle school, especially those in authority positions."

Yes, it does. No one does anything because he or she is forced to do so. Teachers comply with requests of their districts and administrators because they enjoy a tranquil relationship with the principal, the paychecks, and hopefully, the joys of teaching. Middle school students understand this concept well. Students comply with requests because they enjoy the freedoms and privileges that come with establishing trust with their teachers. Students enjoy the benefits of academic success. They enjoy the peace, joy, and happiness that come with complying. Each day, each assignment, each rule, each interaction, and each moment, students make the decision to comply or not comply.

> "Well…what about this topic? Middle school has a bad reputation because a higher percentage of students rebel a lot. When I was in middle school, there were always *those* kids who didn't listen to the teachers almost all the time!"

So, what were *those* kids doing in reality? You used the verb rebel. It's just a label for them because—

> "Because they disagreed! Their version of perfect disagreed with the requests of the school! Oh! I get it now. I understand, but this creates chaos… when so many people disagree. How can peace exist if everyone does only what they really want?"

It actually would bring about world peace. If everyone was doing only what they truly – meaning that desire from way down deep in one's heart that feels so good and exciting and is purely Love - wanted to do, everyone would be happy. Happy people are not angry people. Happy people are filled with peace, happiness, cooperation, and joy. People react negatively when they believe that they cannot have what they want. Enlightening students that they can have anything and everything they want is crucial to middle school peace. Clarifying *how* they can get anything and everything they want is of highest priority! Explaining the benefits of middle school education as one of the many ways they can have anything and everything they want is essential to middle school peace. Having lots of clubs, activities, and special events is vital to middle school peace. Happy middle schoolers are necessary for middle school peace. Schools must make great effort to make environments that foster happy middle schoolers! This begins with explaining they can have anything and everything they truly want.

[SCREAMING COMING FROM YOUR HOUSE. HAIR BEING PULLED OUT.]

OK, I can almost hear your strong reactions, shouting at me about the previous paragraph on middle school peace! So, I will explain further. Many, and I would even say most, kids decide that their idea of perfect is to comply with middle school requests, assignments, rules, and expectations. They mostly are happy to be there and seem to really enjoy middle school. It has purpose and with fun activities, sports, and clubs; they are happy. They are happy because their compliance creates peace, joy, and cooperation in their lives. They are also happy because they see the relationship between what they want and their decisions to succeed in middle school.

Then, there are *those* kids who do not like school. It does not have purpose for them, and it definitely does not fit into their definition of their perfect. They do not see how middle school will give them what they want now or later. Everyone knows that middle school does not agree with their definitions of perfect because they usually show it in many different ways—many of which bring about societal scorn and judgment. There are two options at this point. They can be (seemingly) forced to stay in a place they do not like, or they can be offered alternatives once their true desires are known. Without going too much into school reform (a whole other book!), it is important that all of those involved with middle school aged students be well aware of students' true desires – the ones that feed the pure, positive part of our existences with benefit to all others - so that middle school can be made into a place that agrees with *their* definitions of perfect.

"I am trying to understand this. Really I am, but telling children of any age that they can have anything and everything they truly want? I can't even put words together to describe my concern about this."

A human being's natural state is pure love. All humans crave pure love because that is exactly what they are! The problem is when people do not remember this. Because they do not remember, they feel "off" or "out of sorts" or irritated. Because they feel irritated, they do not treat themselves or others or things with love. All middle school students are pure love and exhibit positive actions when they know this, unless they do not know it or they forget it. All middle school students' natural desires are for peace, joy, and happiness. All middle school students' true desires are respect, success, achievement, and love. Even *those* kids, who do not see the relationship between what is offered by teachers in the form of assignments and what they want out of life...*truly* want: peace, joy, and happiness. True desires for any human being of any age are peace, joy, and happiness. Once everyone understands that everyone is pure love and remembers this, peace, joy, and happiness will exist everywhere.

> "What about the middle school kids who are happy doing vandalism? Hurting others? What about adults who kill? Steal? These people appear happy doing these things! World peace seems so far away and unattainable."

Yes, I agree it does *appear* pretty far out reach, but in reality, it is closer than we realize. So, all human beings must do just that! Realize, or focus, that peace is obtainable, within reach, close, and is our natural state of being – even in middle schools. In other words, each one of us must focus on what makes each one of us happy. I am responsible for my happiness and my happiness only. You are responsible for your happiness and your happiness only. I am to realize and follow my definition of perfect for me. You are to realize your definition of perfect for you. If I do that, I will be happy. If you do that, you will be happy. Broadening this a bit, if everyone in your community focused on his or her happiness and definitions of perfect, then everyone in your community would be happy and a model for world peace.

How does this happen, though? How do we create happy adults? Happy middle schoolers? It starts with creating happy babies, toddlers, three-year-olds, four-year-olds, five-year-olds, six-year-olds…ten-year-olds, eleven-year-olds, twelve-year-olds, and so on. By honoring the perfect wisdom inside each human from the start, happiness abounds!

No one chooses to kill, steal, cheat, lie, vandalize, or hurt from a natural state of happiness. It just cannot be done that way! It *appears* that those doing harm are happy, but they are not. They are doing harm from a place of anger or frustration because they believe that they cannot have everything they want. Malicious human beings have experienced over and over, and have chosen to believe, that they cannot have what they want, so they formed a belief that the only way they can have what they want is to take what they want from those who have it. They demonstrate their frustration by ruining someone else's life. It is so important that we honor the internal wisdom of each human being right from the beginning, encourage each human to discover their individual definition of perfect, and believe that our bountiful, creative, supportive world can provide every single being's definition of perfect. Now, that is positive empowerment!

"Wow. I hadn't thought about it in those terms. That is quite a lot to comprehend and absorb. It's true, though; when I am with people who are all having a good time, all is well and good. Everyone is smiling, laughing, and feeling great. No one is stealing or killing!

You also stated that we can believe that the world can provide everyone's individual definitions of perfect. Do you mean that we are to expect that if we desire it, the world can offer it to us? Everyone could live in a mansion with five cars?"

Yes. Look how the world has provided what we have desired so far! Henry Ford stated a desire to make cars affordable to many. It happened. Then, from Henry Ford's desire, the "many" stated new desires to have variety of motorized vehicles to get us from one place to another. In a little more than two hundred years, we have provided ourselves many more versions of motorized vehicles since Henry Ford's Model T in 1908. Today, we have mopeds, mini bikes, dirt bikes, motorcycles, three-wheelers, four-wheelers, ATVs, SUVs, jet skis, john-boats, motor boats, yachts, mega yachts, cruise liners, and more. We have airplanes and spacecrafts too! The desire and the support for the desire developed, swelled, and enlarged in perfect harmony!

Humans stated the desire to communicate to anyone from anywhere. Life supported us in this so that now many of us have at least one cell phone—a long way from Alexander Graham Bell's desire. Again, the desire and the support for the desire developed, swelled, and enlarged in perfect harmony!

Once Bill Gates' idea for personal computers gathered momentum, people's desire for technology exploded. Life supported this desire with great speed as we now have personal computers, Internet, DVDs, CDs, streaming music, iPods, flat screen TVs, Bluetooth, email, social networking, PC cameras, video conferencing, digital cameras, and more! The desire developed, swelled, and enlarged in perfect harmony!

So, if everyone wanted to live in a mansion with five cars, life would support that too. Life would create a way to make it happen. Remember, great diversity exists, so it is highly unlikely that everyone would want a mansion with five cars. There are people who would not want to be responsible for maintaining a large residence. Some people would not want the daily decision of which car to drive. These things would not be in agreement with their definitions of their perfect.

There are more inventions and more desires to be fulfilled—many, many more yet to come! Yes, there is room for everyone's individual definition of perfect to be created in our world with happiness, peace, joy, and cooperation. Students can experience this during middle school years, and how wonderful for them! What child will disagree when told he can have anything he truly wants? What child would start fussing when told she can have what she truly wants? Would students yell, "No!" at such statements? Um…that is a no brainer! So the question now is why *do* students yell, "No!"? Why does anyone yell, "No!"? People react this way only when they hear or see or experience something that does not agree with their own individual definitions of perfect. When students are told yes, yes, yes about what feels good to them, they will not say no, no, no! It just cannot happen!

> "Well, I can follow the theory and see how life makes space for the increasing desires of humans. But, who will pay for this to happen in all the schools? Our government struggles to pay for public education right now. If we individualized education to that degree, it would cost a fortune."

Yes, it is quite a lot to ponder. It is not a theory, however. This *is* how life supports us and our desires. For a moment, do not look at the logistics (like money) and answer these questions: Does it feel good to you that life supports you in all of your desires? We tell children that they can become anything they want to be. Do we really believe our own words? Perhaps we need to take a look at our beliefs about success. Does it feel good to believe that any desire can become a reality? Yes! Does it feel good to tell children their desires will become their realities? Yes! Would it be great to say, "Yes, let's try that idea of yours right now," to your child? Yes! How about, "I will help you achieve that desire"? Or say to your child, "That incredible thought of yours is doable! We'll make it happen."? Yes! When ideas, thoughts, and desires feel good, life will support them. Even if you cannot see all the way to the end result, believe that it can be done because life will support you. Life will make a path for you. Martin Luther King, Jr. understood this when he said, "Take the first step in faith. You don't have to see the whole staircase. Just take the first step."

TWELVE

Expecting Something Beyond Expecting the Best From Your Child

It is very cliché to state that parents expect the best from their children. Of course, this is true! What does expecting the best really mean, however? Does this mean perfection? Does this mean pushing your child to reach higher and higher goals? Does this mean defeating, surpassing, and rising to the top of all others? Does this mean evaluating what your child is doing on a constant basis? Does it mean proclaiming all possible warnings of what could happen so to avoid the "pit falls" of life? Does expecting the best mean punishing when your child is "off-course" or makes mistakes? Does it mean your child makes no mistakes or should make no mistakes?

I am hoping to provide you with another perspective on expecting the best from your child, because it is more than establishing high standards for your child and monitoring how your child is doing. There is much more. It goes to the "behind the scenes" or the undercurrent energy you are projecting toward your child. Answer these questions honestly to yourself: Do you find yourself wondering what your child is up to when not in your presence? When you have these wonderings, do you automatically think your child might be near trouble or is causing trouble? Do you sneak while checking on your child's activities? Your child's texts? Your child's emails? Your child's notebooks? Your child's phone conversations? Do you warn your child that you are watching him just in case he tries to do anything "crazy"? Do you hint or even announce to your child's teachers that your child is a troublemaker at the parent orientation nights before the school year starts? Do you ask your child's teachers to immediately report any misbehavior to you? Do you find yourself stating detailed pre-warnings, such as informing your daughter that you can check the time her texts are sent so you'll know if she is texting late at night? Or, remind your son as he leaves for school not to skip class before there is a chance for him to do it?

What thought focus do these questions present? Where is the focus pertaining to the child? What feeling is present? How do you feel right now after reading these questions?

> "Um…yeah…I fit into this category. Somehow I don't feel good about it right now. Why? Yes, I <u>*do*</u> check on my child's activities and communications with others without her knowing. I'm being a good parent! I have to be aware of what's going on. This is what good parents do! I have noticed while reading this book that if I wait for your explanation, I get a new positive perspective on things which feels good so I'll wait to see what you got for this one too."

Thanks for the vote of confidence! It is much appreciated. This is what your child wants too. He wants to be given your vote of confidence that he is going to do well, choose positive actions, and succeed. He really is truly only attracted to the positive thoughts, actions, and places in his world. Your son truly wishes to bounce joyfully on life's springy trampoline, run wildly through life's vast wilderness as he intuitively connects with nature, and to bellow loudly from his mountain top. Your daughter truly desires to dance freely with the powerful rhythm of life she intuitively senses pulsing through her body, frolic barefoot in life's wonderful yard, and swim playfully in life's pool of positive possibilities. She naturally wants to blend with, join in, and celebrate together with fun, loving, happy, positive feelings about life!

> "Ooooo…that feels sooo much better! I'd really like to have that with my child all the time! Those are wonderful thoughts and metaphors, but how do they mesh with protecting her and guiding her down a good path?"

It all does mesh, I promise. You can have this all the time. It is a matter of—

> "Don't tell me. I know…focus. It's a matter of my focus. I'm beginning to see and understand how my child's initial success in middle school does depend on me. If I was positive from the start, things would be different now."

Remember, this is a no-guilt book. Absolutely no guilt! Move on from where you are toward where you want to be. No matter what happens, I try to get into the stream of really good feeling vibes as quickly as I can when I realize I am off the mark—the positive mark. I talk with my daughter about when I am not focusing on the positive and model for her how to get back to the flow of the really good feeling vibes, because from this new place I can create my life. It is the "not being in the flow" that makes me realize that I want to be some place different than where I am! It does not feel good out of the flow. In fact, it *really* does not feel good. I get a knot in my stomach to varying degrees. The unwanted feelings sorta shake me awake, like an alarm, to get back to where I really enjoy life, feel good, and desire to be. It is like my spirit talks to me by way of my feelings.

This also works when I am "in" and I get an idea (creation!). If I am really feeling great and get all excited about the idea, then I know I am on the right path for me. I go with the idea and continue on it as long as that good feeling vibe is present. It is like my spirit says to me, "Keep going! Go, Go, GO!!" It is my natural state of being and a great place to live life. It is *everyone's* natural state of being, including middle school students! Pets are in their flows all the time. This is why we feel great just looking at them or petting them. Children are able to find their really good feeling vibes easily, especially babies. We love to be around them, hold them, and sing to them. It is easy to love babies because we enjoy so much being near their flow of really good feeling vibes.

> "Then why would children make decisions that are negative or hurtful if they are in their flows? Some children seem to emanate negativity and are always in trouble."

If children repeatedly see and experience others focusing on something else besides getting in and staying in the flow, children can choose to ignore their own positive vibrations. Look at these metaphors again with added clarifying text:

"He really is truly only attracted to the positive thoughts, actions, and places in his world. Your son truly wishes to bounce joyfully on life's springy trampoline, run wildly through life's vast wilderness as he intuitively connects with nature, and to bellow loudly from his mountain top *unless he consistently is shown the opposite and chooses to follow the opposite*. Your daughter truly desires to dance freely with the powerful rhythm of life she intuitively senses pulsing through her body, frolic barefoot in life's wonderful yard, and swim playfully in life's pool of positive possibilities. She naturally wants to blend with, join in, and celebrate together with fun, loving, happy, positive feelings about life *unless she sees a model that shows her to focus on the negative possibilities of life and chooses to believe in those possibilities."*

> "How is anyone not supposed to feel guilty right now? Every parent has probably done that! Every parent probably has looked at, talked about, and warned against life's negative situations. That's what a parent is supposed to do!"

Look once more at the metaphors.

"He really is truly only attracted to the positive thoughts, actions, and places in his world. Your son truly wishes to bounce joyfully on life's springy trampoline, run wildly through life's vast wilderness as he intuitively connects with nature, and to bellow loudly from his mountain top unless he consistently is shown the opposite and chooses to follow the opposite. Your daughter truly desires to dance freely with the powerful rhythm of life she intuitively senses pulsing through her body, frolic barefoot in life's wonderful yard, and swim playfully in life's pool of positive possibilities. She naturally wants to blend with, join in, and celebrate together with fun, loving, happy, positive feelings about life unless she sees modeling of focusing on the negative possibilities of life and chooses to believe in those possibilities."

Ultimately, the final decisions about our lives, anyone's life, your life, your child's life, rest with the individual's personal choice. There is no parental guilt! Children make their own decisions. Parents do, however, have a huge impact and influence on their children. It can be an awesome and wonderful influence filled with much love, peace, joy, positive modeling, humor, acceptance, and communal learning. Or, it cannot. Or, it can be a combination of both. Which do you prefer? Now that you may be aware of your impact on your child, you can decide to live in your flow of your really good feeling vibes and model that kind of living so that it reminds your child who he really is and how he can live his life in his flow. It will make you feel really good to know that you are guiding your child in this direction. How will you know if she is in her flow? She will display happiness, peacefulness, and energy! How will he know he is in his flow? He will feel happy, peaceful, and energetic! The negative exists to assist him to get back in his flow. We all will know if we are in our individual flows (or not) by our feelings!

> "So if I, as a parent, focus on the positives of life and discuss the positives of the events of my life, and if he naturally desires the good stuff of life, like running wildly through life's vast wilderness, why would he choose negative actions at times?"

He may forget about the good feelings and the best place to create one's life. By getting out of the flow, one realizes that one was formerly in the flow and now wants to return to the flow, and that it was a really good place!

> "Huh?"

As discussed earlier, how can we know up unless we know down? Knowing *there* teaches *here*. Feeling cold makes one appreciate hot. Being out of the flow of really good feeling vibes broadens one's perspective of just how wonderful it was to be "in." So by realizing the purpose of the opposite of positive exists to support us, parents can release the "obligation" of shining a light on the negative! By understanding this simple, yet very powerful truth about our world, parents can be released of having to warn and focus on the negatives of life.

Plus, it is exhausting to do so! Making negative statements prior to them possibly happening is focusing on what could go wrong. Gosh! If some parents want to continue this way of parenting, they sure have a huge job before them! They will have to think of or know about every possible "trouble" in order to tell their children that they (the parents) will be watching to be sure he or she will not do them. What about the "troubles" they have not thought about? And, always having to be watching out for negatives? Now, that is a tough parenting job! No thanks. This way of interacting with children actually empowers the potentially negative actions to happen. What message does this send to children? Trust? Nope. Support? Nope. What parents focus on is what they are bringing toward them…fast. None of this feels very good to me. If it does not feel good, it cannot be good. It feels out of the flow to me.

So, what is expecting the best from a child really? To answer this, parents must first analyze the beliefs they hold about children. Is parenting shining a light on the good or shining a light on the "evil" in your child? Are human beings good or bad, or a combination of both? No matter your perspective, what do you want to focus on? The truth is if parents expect the best from their children, they will more than likely get the best. If parents warn children that they (the children) are being watched in case something is done wrong, something done wrong is more than likely the result. If children are pre-threatened with consequences about negative actions that haven not happened yet, the negative actions will more than likely be done. Children do not want to misbehave, but do so to get attention, when someone gives them ideas, or they believe misbehaving is what children do or are supposed to do. When a parent threatens consequences for actions that have not happened yet, is that parent giving the child mischievous ideas? Is the parent saying: I expect you to misbehave and I am watching for when you are going to do it? None of this feels good to me. If it does not feel good, it cannot be good. It feels out of the flow to me.

Instead, parents can believe that children want to do well all the time. Parents can believe that all children have their own pure internal wisdom to guide them. Parents can believe that all children sense and feel the positive or negative of their choices. So, to state these affirmatively: All children are wonderful creations filled with their individual perfect wisdoms, which guide them toward satisfying, creative, loving, and happy lives. This statement feels soooo much better! But, it is pretty radical, right?

> "Yes, it is! Whoa! It's like you are saying that children are perfect and don't make mistakes. There is no way you can support this. My children make mistakes all the time. It's a good thing I am watching at them!"

It is not that I am advocating staying away from your child or not being involved with all aspects of your child's life. When children are young, it is the parent's job to be sure they are safe. We guide and keep them safe as they begin their Earthly lives. We tell them the "guidelines" of Earthly living. For example: "You need air to breathe and water does not provide that, so when around water you must be able to keep your head above water where the air is." Or, "You have a soft body with bones that can only withstand so much pressure, so stay here on this street curb with me and hold my hand so that we are not in the same place as a moving car." Or for older kids, "That person who said those mean things to you does not feel good about himself. It is not about you; it is about him. Why would someone say mean things? Because he does not feel good inside. What are your options to turn this situation around to a good feeling situation?"

~

Be a Positively Involved Parent

Be involved! Be aware! Know what your child is doing at all times, but do it with positive energy. Go through your child's emails, texts, on-line communication with friends, and so on, *with* your child. Have her explain who each friend is and how she knows the person. If you see or read something that feels negative to you, discuss it with your child. Ask her how the communication feels to her. This will sharpen your daughter's ability to listen to her feelings—communication from her spirit. Have your son explain a text conversation to you as you look at the texts together. Discuss all communication between your child and peers. Explain if some do not feel positive to you and why. Ask the child to tell you how it feels to him. Expect that your child is capable of making healthy decisions. When you sense something that is not positive, discuss your concerns. Explain why you put a parental control (I want this renamed to Positively Focused Internet!) on the computer. Is it that you do not trust your child, or you do not trust the Internet? Explain that the parental control is selecting only positive and useful Web sites. The parental control narrows the search (focus) of the Internet sites so that they are all for students. In this way, the parental control *assists* the child instead of restricts the child!

Just what are "mistakes" that kids make? What are mistakes that adults make? What are mistakes that anyone makes? Mistakes are actions that are not in the direction of where the person wants to go. Mistakes are actions that create results that do not feel good. Mistakes are learning opportunities. Mistakes are wonderful and useful life tools. Mistakes are not in agreement with who the person says they are. Mistakes say, "I'm off my course." Mistakes are made when a person is not in his or her "personal positive good feeling flow."

Are mistakes bad? Are mistakes good? It depends the way one looks at mistakes. I see them as positive opportunities to evaluate who I am and where I want to go from my current time, place, and status. If I do something and the result does not feel good, then I can tell that the action is in the wrong direction for me. If someone else does the same action and it feels good, then the action is going in the right direction for them. For example, one time at a high school youth camp, we (about 350 campers) were being entertained by a bunch of leaders pretending to be rock stars. The group of girls I was with decided to go up front and pretend we were cheering for them as if it was a real rock concert. Somehow, I was line leader for this group of girls and I went right on the stage because that is what I thought the rest of the group was going to do! I quickly got off the stage when I saw my peers at the base of the stage. This action was a mistake for me...a definite mistake because I felt everyone saw me and knew I messed up. I had a knot in my stomach for two days! An extrovert would view it differently and would not have seen it as a mistake. An extrovert would have stayed up on the stage, danced, and loved the experience!

So, what is a mistake? Is a mistake when it hurts someone else's feelings? Is it a mistake when it breaks a law? How many people do you know who speed while driving their cars? If they speed, they are breaking the law. Is it a mistake only if the police give speeding tickets? My definition of a mistake is when an action makes me feel weird, uncomfortable, strange, and negative. My spirit will let me know when I am out of my own personal positive good feeling flow or off my own course. My own course...not someone else's course. I know that I can always choose another action, another path, another way to handle a situation if previous actions got me results that did not make me feel one hundred percent great. With this definition of mistake, one can look at other's actions with new understanding and new patience.

"Wow. That's a pretty different definition of mistake from the one I am using and was taught as a young child. I can see how your definition frees everyone from blame since mistakes are learning experiences rather than actions to be punished."

No matter your definition of mistake, what do you want to focus on? What focus will get the best from your child? What focus will elicit positive vibes from your child? If you focus on your child's mistakes, you will get plenty of them. If you focus on your child's positives, you will get plenty of them. If you focus on both your child's mistakes and positives, you will get plenty of them. Which scenario creates the most positive situation with your child?

I am not writing that you will never see your child's mistakes. Oh, you will see mistakes. What do you do about what you see? Can you handle the mistakes positively? Yes, you can! With this approach, you are focusing only on the positives. For example, your child says something perceived as mean to another student at school. You get a call from a school administrator about the incident. *You* now have many choices! Do you get embarrassed, furious, mad, or angry? Do you have control over your emotion choices? Yes, you do. Which ones will you choose? If you believe that your child made a mistake and is supposed to do as you have taught him, then embarrassed, furious, mad, or angry might be your choice. If you believe that your child made a mistake and you want to find out how the action made him feel, you may feel hopeful and curious. Later, when talking to your child about the incident, you find out all the details and how your child felt about his action. If it was a situation of standing up for him or herself, then perhaps your child feels great and empowered (in the flow). If it was a situation of trying to overpower another child, then perhaps your child senses a stomach knot (not in the flow). List with your child the choices for handling future interactions with the child. Allow your child to give you choices of actions. Add to the list, if needed. Show that there are many choices to choose. Which ones feel good? Which ones will get the desired result? Discuss it until everyone feels good.

> "That's good! I really like it. But, what about those kids who don't seem to have a grip on their emotions? What about the ones who seem to feel great when hurting another?"

Those kids have repeatedly seen and experienced denying one's pure, natural feelings. It is difficult to view such events with compassion, but that is exactly what is needed. Some children have not been encouraged to sense their true feelings and to pay attention to their feelings—their guide. They have not been shown that there is a flow of really good feeling vibes available to them by focusing on things that make them truly happy. They have not had the opportunity to have their feelings honored...yet. With compassion, love, and understanding, all students can learn to choose good feelings.

With some kids, this is a process. They have been experiencing and staying in bad moods for long periods of time. Jumping from their current emotion to happy just is not going to happen. People who experience depression know that sometimes they "can't even get a whiff of bliss,"[11] as Abraham-Hicks states. People can choose to gradually move into better and better feeling emotions. This means, however, that someone who is depressed will first go through the heavier emotions of anger, revenge, and frustration before reaching some lighter and more positive emotions of hope, trust, joy, love, and belief.

> "Are you saying that anger is better than depression? I'd rather have depressed people than angry people around me. Depressed people are safer."

Well, what is depression? Depression—decoded: de (down) + pres (to hold) + sion (state of being)—means to hold down one's state of being. In other words, it is when a person shoves and locks his or her emotions into a box so that the emotions are not available. People do this for many reasons, such as severe traumatic experiences or extended periods of time feeling helpless. Depression is lifted, literally, when a person unlocks the box and takes a look at what is inside.[12] When a person makes the brave and powerful choice to deal with those de-pressed feelings, a surge of emotion is released from the box and is now available to that person again. Which emotion is released? Happiness? Not quite because happiness is nowhere near what that person is feeling. The released emotion is usually anger—anger at what made the person shove and lock the emotions in the box in the first place. Often, at this point, the people surrounding the recovering depressed person don't like it because the depressed person is utilizing the emotion of anger and evidence of this is quite obvious.[13] As long as the depressed person, now angry person, keeps moving through the emotions popping out of the box to the ones that feel good, life will get better for everyone. However, there are some people who stay stuck in one or a few particular negative emotions. This is when compassion is exactly what is needed to encourage the formerly depressed and now angry or frustrated person to move to the next better feeling emotion he or she can release from the box...over and over again...all the way to joy and love and happiness.

So those who seem to be happy doing negative actions appear this way because they are feeling better since moving from depression to anger or frustration. These people *do* feel better! Compassion will assist them toward the great feelings. From a place of happiness, peace, and joy, people will not hurt others.

Healing the Past

The positive lists of middle school will greatly assist with this very thing. If a negative situation occurs, a child has two options: to feel empowered or to feel helpless. With compassionate help, a child can turn the situation around to feel empowered instead of feeling helpless. Remember, this works for the past too. At any time, anyone can take another look at any negative situation and release the anger or frustration from the situation. For example, I had a friend in college, who was domineering and moody. It was very frustrating because I felt helpless, angry, and manipulated by her. Unfortunately, I endured the situation to keep the peace with her and others involved. Eventually, I promised myself to make no more commitments with this "friend" after graduation. That promise was my first effort to reach for a better feeling emotion because it was the first time I addressed my helplessness. So I went from helplessness to starting the empowering process in my life, and it felt good.

But, this was not enough. I still had many negative feelings locked in my box, even after graduation. Eventually I released them one by one until I was able to have peace about the situation. My friend taught me many things for which I am now thankful. I now recognize overbearing people and have the skills to handle such personalities. She taught me how to stand up for myself because I spent much time in the years following graduation analyzing my inability in college to do so. I now enjoy speaking my truth when it truly feels good to me, which is independent of the opinions and reactions of others. In other words, I feared her reactions and the reactions of those involved with our "friendship" more than I wanted my feelings to count. Now, I enjoy knowing my true thoughts, opinions, and feelings are the only things I need to honor. If it feels good to me to listen to or discuss other's opinions and feelings, then I will, but only if it feels good to me first. This is quite a shift! Even with graduation a memory of the past, I can turn around my feelings toward this person and find peace about that time in my life. So, now I say, "Thank you!"

~

Getting In and Out of Trouble at School

Here is another personal example. My daughter was having a period of time at school when she perceived she was getting picked on by teachers and other adults in the building. She was reprimanded about her electronic device. She was "caught" twice by two different teachers on the same day for the same reason, even though all year long her teachers sang her praises. The principal even negatively addressed her during this time! All three incidences were within a few days of each other, so when the third day came around, I discussed with her what was going on and her choices for how to improve things.

Did she know why she was appearing to get in trouble a lot at school? She replied because the teachers were grumpy. I asked her several questions about the school's policy regarding the "issues" she was having. By doing this, I could see that my daughter knew the school expectations and no further clarification was needed. If she did not know, we could consider researching the school policies as one of the possible choices on her "My Options" list.

Next, could she identify why so many incidents were happening so close together and why they were happening at all when she rarely had any negative interactions with teachers or administrators? After some thought, the grumpy teacher idea came out again. I asked her what her thoughts were about school since it was getting close to the end of the school year. Was she thinking about getting out for the summer? Was she thinking about being able to do whatever she wanted during the summer? Did she have any resentment that she was still in school? Although not very strong thoughts and emotions, she did have these focuses hanging around her.

Through our conversation, she began to notice how her thoughts and feelings were impacting her daily life because why would two different teachers' focuses be on her the same day for something negative when their focus had been previously all positive for the months and months prior? Could it be because she was projecting negativity about them and school? Of all the hundreds of places the principal could have been that one morning when he observed her using her electronic device after the allotted time in the morning, he just happened to be standing near her at the very moment she pulled it from her pocket? She just happened to be in his line of vision when he could have been facing away from her? I asked, "What are the chances?" She pondered these things. "Do you think you are attracting these situations?"

A smile appeared on her face as she realized she was making these apparent negative situations happen. The smile was one of empowerment! If she could make the situations happen, she could make them go away too. She could make positive interactions happen just like she had all year. We discussed her choices and options to create a new reality for her. Yes, these were not major negative events, but it was still wonderful, awesome, successful, and thrilling for her to feel her own power to determine the reality she preferred in her life. It was still wonderful, awesome, successful, and thrilling for me to assist with her empowerment so that these little issues stopped before becoming regular occurrences. Do you see how child empowerment empowers parents too?

> "I noticed that in your communication with your daughter, you used questioning. Is this because you want the answers… or insight…or understanding… to come from her rather than you?"

Yes. The questions are very much asked on purpose. No child just wants to be told what to do. By asking questions, it prompted her to seek the answers from within herself. The discovery was hers. I was only the facilitator.

FYI: Happy People Are…Happy!

Imagine a world where everyone is smiling, feeling joy, and is happy. If everyone feels good, what is the result? Hitting? Yelling? Anger? No! Do people perform negative actions when happy? No! If everyone feels good, the result is peace, joy, contentment, love, and compassion. I have been saying for years, "Nice people are nice for a reason. Mean people are mean for a reason." How can we get all human beings to feel good all the time? It starts with shining a spotlight on the positive. So…

Thank your child often for reaching for the best he or she can be. Thank your child often for table manners. Thank your child for learning so well. Thank your child for not laughing when so and so's zipper was down. Thank your child for maintaining his dignity when his team lost the championship. Thank your daughter for exhibiting confidence and maturity when those around her were gossiping. Thank your child for attracting nice friends. Thank your child for that cute nose, or being beautiful on the outside and the inside, or putting the book bag near the front door before going to bed, or for being so funny, or for smiling, or for drinking a milkshake without noises, or putting dishes into the dishwasher, or…. Thank your child for whatever he or she has done that is positive. Thank often and thank specifically.

Thank your son for being your son. Thank your daughter for being your daughter. Thank your child for bringing joy to your life, for being so handsome or cute, for writing neatly, for taking a telephone message while you were gone, for sweeping the floors, for eating lunch, for getting up on time, for...anything positive!

Thank your child for cleaning grandma's house, or remembering her social studies book this evening, or being able to do a handstand, or being able to ride a bike so well. Thank your child for the wonderful hug, for getting you a glass of milk just now, for wearing matching clothes, for being a fun pre-teenie or teenager, or being able to walk away from an unwanted friendship, or waiting for a shopping trip to the mall, or for volunteering to babysit, or whatever you are want to shine a spotlight on to create more of it!

Not comfortable with saying positive comments? Start with yourself privately in the mirror. State positives only. Look at yourself in the mirror and say anything positive that comes to the surface of your mind, such as, "You have nice ears. I like my nose. You are funny. I am working on becoming the person I want to be. I like feeling good. I think my toes are cute." Work your way up to saying, "I love you." And, "I love you, ___________ (your name in blank)." Louise Hay, author and founder of Hay House Publishing, has an absolutely fascinating story of how she used self-affirmations to bring her power back to herself. She healed herself physically, emotionally, and spiritually through much mirror affirmation talk.[14] If saying positive comments to others is difficult, start with yourself because you gotta have the love inside of you first in order to give it to others.

Here is another idea: give yourself a kiss. Yup! That is right. A kiss! Do you feel worthy of kisses from yourself? These are really special and powerful kisses. As silly as it may sound, work your way up to loving yourself to the point you can blow a kiss to yourself in the mirror. Blow lively and playful kisses to yourself or kiss the back of your hand. It will transform your life! Kiss your arms with quick, silly kisses as you would a newborn baby. Feel the love emanating from yourself to yourself! Feel the silliness! Feel the joy! Laugh if you want to! Because this is done in your privacy, this is a wonderful gift to give yourself. It will rock your world!

Ever self-hug? I would place huge bets that you have done this especially when crying. Often people bend their knees, bring them into their chests, wrap their arms around their knees, and place their heads on their knees when upset. It is a self-hug! We do this without thinking. Often people will get into "fetal" position when crying. Self-hugging is similar since while lying down the knees are brought up toward the chest, the shoulders are rounded, and the arms embrace the bent legs. You do not have to be upset or crying to give yourself a hug. By wrapping your arms around your neck, your chest, or your middle, you can give yourself a wonderful dosage of pure love. Squeeze tight and release! You can even make that verbal hugging noise to go with your hugs. Try it now and see just how great it feels!

Still not comfortable saying positive comments to others? There are other ways to let your child know that you are looking at and for the positives. Try these on your child: give a pat on the back, or a thumbs up hand signal, mail a letter or note, put a note in your child's lunch, write a note in your child's agenda for today's date *and* random future dates, make a card and send it, purchase a card and send it, put a note under your child's pillow, place a sticky note on the bathroom mirror, put a note in a drawer used daily by your child, make a treasure hunt of positive notes throughout the house, put a note in his soccer cleats, put a note in piano books, create a mobile of positives for her room, or take your child shopping just because.

Working Toward the Perfect Definition of You

OK, so you started on this positive journey with your middle school child and you messed up. You said something negative and your child let you know his disapproval of it. How does he feel? How do you feel? Not so good? Great! You are both aware of how you feel and now have a starting place to change! That knot in your stomach is a wonderful thing because it is letting you know that you are "off-course." It is saying, "Hey! You are going in a direction you told me you did not want to go. So let's turn around, OK? Try again with a positive comment. You can do it!"

This is also a great time to model for your child how to make a new decision for your life. With a calm voice, "__________ (your child's name), I have realized that I am focusing too much on negative things and I am in the process of choosing to be positive. I will probably mess up from time to time as I get to where I want to be. Please be patient with me." Your child will most likely look at you strangely, but in time, she will learn to trust the change in you. What a wonderful gift to give to yourself and your child!

If you are just awakening to the fact that you need to implement this strategy into your relationship with your child (and it works with any of your relationships), do so right away! As parents move away from threats, negative comments, or sneakiness, children naturally respond. As parents move toward appreciation, thankfulness, and trust, children naturally respond! Depending on the degree negative communication has been used and the degree positive communication will be implemented, children will respond to the change at different paces. Be patient! Keep being positive! Notice and put a spotlight only on what your child is doing well. Turn any mistakes into opportunities to seek the best from your child. Create lists of choices together. The tremendous, peaceful reward will serve you both for many, many years to come. Expect the best from your child!

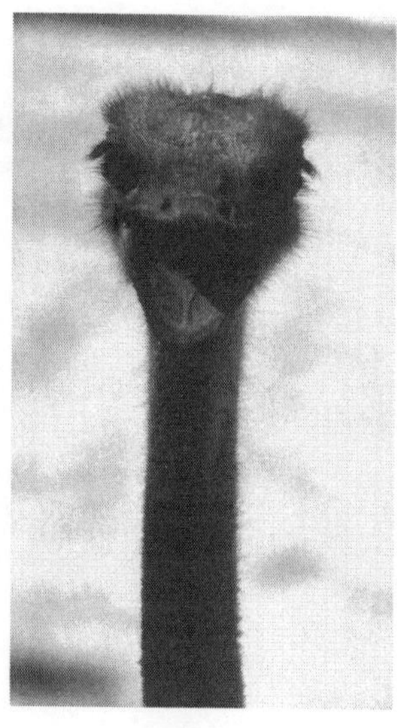

EPILOGUE

It is not that I have my head stuck in the sand about reality. (By the way, did you know that ostriches do not stick their heads in sand?) I see, feel, hear, and sense the effects of all of humanity's collective focus and thoughts all too well. I know people have many things in their lives they do not like. At this point, we all have two options. We can continue as is and focus on what is wrong and what we do not like, which will bring about more of the same. Or, we can focus on what we would like, those things that we love, and what brings us feelings of joy, which will bring about positive change. I have made huge positive changes in my life through this method. I have read about and witnessed other people making huge positive changes in their lives through this method too. I have witnessed people attracting the very things they talk about, whether they are positive or negative—that is what they get! In fact, it is quite easy to see this in other people. Look at another's life. What are they attracting? How are they attracting it? Proof of positive attracts positive and negative attracts negative is everywhere. Now you know the power for good living! Use it! Feel it! Enjoy an awesome life!

I am not alone in understanding this and experiencing the positive effects. Take a look at this collection of people who embraced this simple understanding about life as I found in Rhonda Byrnes' phenomenal book, The Secret1 [15]:

"All that we are is a result of what we have thought."
-Buddha (563 BCE – 483 BCE)

"What things soever ye desire, when ye pray*, believe that ye receive them, and ye shall have them."
-Jesus of Nazareth (4 BCE – 30 AD) Mark 11:24
*Focus could replace the word pray, couldn't it?

"See the things that you want as already yours. Know that they will come to you at need. Then let them come."
-Robert Collier (1885 – 1950)

"It is the combination of thought and love which forms the irresistible force of the law of attraction."
-Charles Haanel (1866 – 1949)

"That a man can change himself...and master his own destiny is the conclusion of every mind who is wide-awake to the power of right thought."
-Christian D. Larson (1866-1954)

"You create your own universe as you go along."
-Winston Churchill (1874 – 1965)

"Imagination is everything. It is the preview of life's coming attractions."
-Albert Einstein (1879 – 1955)

"Whatever the mind...can conceive it can achieve."
-W. Clement Stone (1902 – 2002)

"Whether you think you can or think you can't, either way you are right."
-Henry Ford (1863–1947)

If we really look at the effective leaders of the past, we will see that they set an example for us of how to make change occur. They all did it with the power of their visions, dreams, and positive thoughts.

Positive change IS happening! It is because humanity is believing in its own power. It is believing in the goodness of life. It is believing that true peace is obtainable. It is believing in the connection we have with each other. Technological advances have assisted in making this available to us. I implore you to see the wonder in all of life from your ability to move a finger, to all the hands that made your furniture, to the diversity of the universe. I implore you to appreciate the smile on a passerby's face, the manners of the person holding a door for you, the determination of a bird looking for worms, the giggle of a baby, the cracks in the sidewalk from a tree's insistence of rightful territory, the ever changing beautiful cloud formations in the sky, the earth's ability to provide a stable environment for life, and the splendor of the starry show at night.

I implore you to smile when you see your middle school student "spazz" for no particular reason, when your middle school child gets a zit, when your middle school child says middle schoolish words like "So coooollll" and "Duuuuuddde," when your child comes home from school with a green inked hand, when your child burps, when your child wears clothes that do not match, when your child jumps up and down in front of you for what seems like infinity, when your child falls asleep doing homework, when your child thinks so and so is cute, when your child wants to play basketball instead of doing homework, when your child wants longer hair than you would like, when your child wants to meet friends at the mall, when your male child comes home from school with five or more short pigtails because he allowed some girls to put numerous rubber bands in his hair, when your child wants to have friends sign her shirt at the end of the year, or when your child does anything that reminds you that he or she is in middle school. Focusing positively on all of these things, quite simply, benefits all. Keep this focus and you will find your entire life peaceful. It will naturally spread to others. It will spread from your neck of the woods all the way to the edges of the universe and back to the hallways of your child's middle school, even before he or she gets there. These are not mere words. Think it. Feel it. Believe it. Experience it.

I am filled with gratitude for those who attracted this book into their existences. It is by no chance that this occurred. I desire to attract those who want to understand the power of positive energy, and those who already embrace this power. There may be those who will scoff at the simplicity of positive thinking. I understand, because sometimes it is really tough to see the light of day through difficulties. But, I keep returning to this one point: Which feels better? To keep on thinking about what is wrong, or to think about what would be awesome? As for me, I will be thinking about the fact that I can have more, about what I want in life, about peace, and about positive experiences in middle school. How about you?

Hopefully, you feel empowered to proactively assist your child to the middle school doorstep with the many suggestions and strategies to implement before the first day of school. I stick to my claim that the initial success of your child in middle school depends on you, the parent. I hope that this claim no longer threatens you, but invigorates you and makes you already feel successful in your parental role!

Do you understand that most of the middle school preparation is not about *doing* something? Most of the preparation for middle school is about *feeling* your way to a wonderful, awesome, successful, and thrilling middle school experience. It is about parents projecting goodness regarding middle school to their children, which will, hopefully, encourage those children to decide to project goodness regarding middle school inside the building's hallways, classrooms, cafeteria, bathrooms, lockers, locker rooms, desks, books, book bags, assignments, papers, pencils, activities, clubs, administrators, teachers, school nurses, receptionists, bookkeepers, day porters, media center specialists, and, of course, their peers.

So, stand tall, stand proud, and stand confident as you take your ten to fourteen-year-old child to school and watch him get on the middle school roller coaster ride with such tremendous enthusiasm as only a child of this age can exhibit. These next few years are an exhilarating ride. It is a fantastic time in her life, and <u>yes, you now believe</u> that it can be a wonderful, awesome, successful, and thrilling experience!

ENDNOTES

1. Swanson, Rose Marie. Certified Spiritual Counselor, www.akashic-darshan.com.
2. Neena Samuel, "13 Things Your Child's Teacher Won't Tell You," *Reader's Digest*, October 2009.
3. Joe Vitale, *The Attractor Factor: 5 Easy Steps for Creating Wealth (Or Anything Else) From The Inside Out* (Hoboken: John Wiley & Sons, Inc., 2005).
4. Michael Murphy, *Positive Attitudes.com*, www.positiveattitudes.com.
5. Joe Vitale in *The Secret*, Rhonda Byrne (New York: Atria Books, 2006), 149-150; and Jerry and Esther Hicks with Abraham, compact disc, San Antonio, TX-B, November 17, 2007, www.abraham-hicks.com/lawofattractionsource/index.php.
6. Jerry and Esther Hicks with Abraham, compact disc, San Diego, CA, August 23, 2008, www.abraham-hicks.com/lawofattraction-source/in dex.php.
7. Jerry and Esther Hicks with Abraham, compact disc, Asheville, NC, October 23, 2005, www.abraham-hicks.com/lawofattraction-source/index.php.
8. Barbara J. Borom, PhD, Counselor, professional consultation, 2000, www.spiritabundant.com.
9. Kim Jenkins, "Mojo Monday: Manifesting Desires with A 10/10 Journal," Owning Pink, www.owningpink.com/2009/11/30/mojo-monday-manifesting-desires-with-a-1010-journal.
10. "Job Shadow," Job Shadow Coalition & JA Worldwide, www.job-shadow.org.
11. Jerry and Esther Hicks with Abraham, compact disc, Orlando, FL, November 10, 2007, www.abraham-hicks.com/lawofattraction-source/index.php.

12. Barbara J. Borom, PhD, Counselor, professional consultation, 2000, www.spiritabundant.com.
13. Jerry and Esther Hicks with Abraham, compact disc, Detroit, MI, September 22, 2009, www.abraham-hicks.com/lawofattractionsource/index.php.
14. Louise L. Hay, *You Can Heal Your Life*, (Carlsbad, CA: Hay House, Inc. 1984), 220-221.
15. Rhonda Byrne, *The Secret,* (New York: Atria Books, 2006).

REFERENCES

I have personally read or listened to all of these sources and whole heartedly offer them as positive, empowering reads. As you review this list, notice a "switch" or a "flip" or a funny feeling coming from your belly area. This feeling is your indication that *your* book angel is telling you to pursue that source of information and that the contents would be in your highest good!

God Wears Lipstick by Karen Berg

A Woman's Journey to God by Joan Borysenko, Ph.D.
Fire in the Soul by Joan Borysenko, Ph.D.

The Secret by Rhonda Byrne
The Secret Gratitude Book by Rhonda Byrne
The Power by Rhonda Byrne

Don't Sweat the Small Stuff for Teens by Richard Carlson

"The Wayne Dyer CD Collection" by Dr. Wayne Dyer (audio)

Embraced By the Light by Betty J. Eadie
The Awakening Heart: My Continuing Journey to Love by Betty J. Eadie
The Ripple Effect by Betty J. Eadie

The Hidden Messages in Water by Dr. Masaru Emoto

Why Good People Do Bad Things by Debbie Ford

Eat, Pray, Love by Elizabeth Gilbert

The One Minute Millionaire by Mark Victor Hansen & Robert G. Allen

You Can Heal Your Life by Louise Hay

Ask and It Is Given by Esther and Jerry Hicks
The Law of Attraction by Esther and Jerry Hicks
The Vortex by Esther and Jerry Hicks
Sara, Book 1 by Esther and Jerry Hicks

Think and Grow Rich by Napoleon Hill

The Precious Present by Spencer Johnson, M.D.

The Dance of the Dissident Daughter by Sue Monk Kidd

Busting Loose From the Money Game by Robert Scheinfeld

The Power of Now by Eckhart Tolle.

Conversations with God, Book One by Neale Donald Walsh
Conversations with God, Book Two by Neale Donald Walsh
Conversations with God, Book Three by Neale Donald Walsh
Friendship with God by Neale Donald Walsh
Communion with God by Neale Donald Walsh
Happier Than God by Neale Donald Walsh
Home with God In A Life That Never Ends by Neale Donald Walsh
What God Wants by Neale Donald Walsh
Question and Answers to Conversations with God by Neale Donald Walsh
The New Revelations by Neale Donald Walsh

The Attractor Factor by Dr. Joe Vitale

PHOTO CREDITS

1. John Lennon Page: Lizabeth S. Jenkins-Dale - Strawberry Fields in Central Park, Manhattan, NY
2. Introduction: Jeffrey S. Dale – Hershey Park, Hershey, PA
3. Chapter One: Jeffrey S. Dale – Charleston Harbor, Charleston, SC
4. Chapter Two: Jeffrey S. Dale – Central Market, York, PA
5. Chapter Three: Jeffrey S. Dale – Middle School Student
6. Chapter Four: Jeffrey S. Dale – Folly Beach Pier, Folly Beach, SC
7. Chapter Five: Jeffrey S. Dale – Flower
8. Chapter Six: Lizabeth S. Jenkins-Dale – Cake
9. Chapter Seven: Jeffrey S. Dale - Clouds
10. Chapter Eight: Jeffrey S. Dale – Devils Tower National Monument, WY
11. Chapter Nine: Lizabeth S. Jenkins-Dale – Statue of Liberty, Liberty Island, NY
12. Chapter Ten: Jeffrey S. Dale – Charleston Harbor, Charleston, SC
13. Chapter Eleven: Jeffrey S. Dale – Greenfield Village, Dearborn, MI
14. Chapter Twelve: Lizabeth S. Jenkins-Dale – Glacier National Park, MT
15. Epilogue: Jeffrey S. Dale – Detroit Zoo, Detroit, MI

5168334R00118

Made in the USA
San Bernardino, CA
27 October 2013